JOHN WILHELM 1

John Wilhelm Rowntree (1890's)

John Wilhelm Rowntree
1868 - 1905

and the beginnings of modern Quakerism

'the man who doubts,
the man who dares to soar'
J.W.R. 1904

by
Stephen Allott

Sessions Book Trust
York, England

ISBN 1 85072 137 8

Printed in 10 on 11 point Plantin Typeface
by William Sessions Limited
The Ebor Press
York, England

Sources and Acknowledgements

ESSAYS AND ADDRESSES may still be found in Meeting House libraries, and this, and *Palestine Notes*, also edited by Joshua Rowntree, remain the chief sources for the life and writings of John Wilhelm Rowntree. For further material one must search in the Quaker periodicals of the time and in Quaker archives. I am most grateful for the help I have received from Malcolm Thomas, Librarian of Friends House Library; Christina Lawson, Librarian of Woodbrooke; Elizabeth Jackson, Librarian of the Joseph Rowntree Foundation; Clifford Smith, Archivist of Bootham School and Mary Hoxie Jones of Haverford, Pennsylvania.

I am indebted to Thomas C. Kennedy's *History and the Quaker Renaissance: the vision of John Wilhelm Rowntree* (Haverford College Quaker Collection), and I have gathered valuable sidelights from Elizabeth Gray Vining's *Friend of Life* (Rufus Jones), Phoebe Doncaster's *John Stephenson Rowntree*, S. E. Robson's *Joshua Rowntree*, Anne Vernon's *A Quaker Business Man* (Joseph Rowntree), and Elfrida Vipont's *Arnold Rowntree*.

I am particularly grateful for the loan of some photographs from Jean Wilhelma Rowntree and her help and encouragement. She is John Wilhelm's youngest daughter, whose friendship with Mary Hoxie Jones has continued the friendship of their fathers and preserved an important oral tradition.

Contents

Illustrations

*Courtesy Joseph Rowntree Foundation
†Courtesy Jean Wilhelma Rowntree
‡Courtesy Quaker Collection, Haverford College, USA

Simplified Rowntree Genealogy

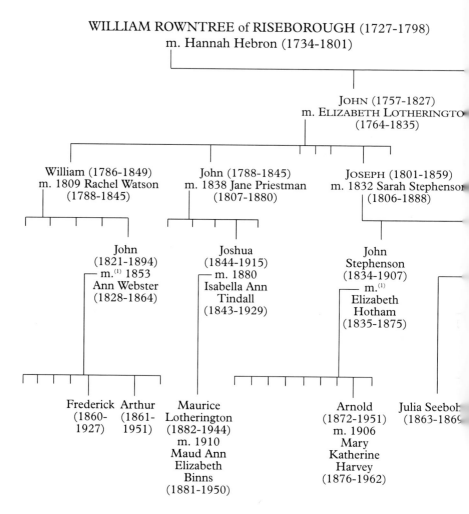

WILLIAM ROWNTREE of RISEBOROUGH (1727-1798)
m. Hannah Hebron (1734-1801)

JOHN (1757-1827)
m. ELIZABETH LOTHERINGTON
(1764-1835)

William (1786-1849)
m. 1809 Rachel Watson
(1788-1845)

John (1788-1845)
m. 1838 Jane Priestman
(1807-1880)

JOSEPH (1801-1859)
m. 1832 Sarah Stephenson
(1806-1888)

John
(1821-1894)
m.(1) 1853
Ann Webster
(1828-1864)

Joshua
(1844-1915)
m. 1880
Isabella Ann
Tindall
(1843-1929)

John
Stephenson
(1834-1907)
m.(1)
Elizabeth
Hotham
(1835-1875)

Frederick
(1860-
1927)

Arthur
(1861-
1951)

Maurice
Lotherington
(1882-1944)
m. 1910
Maud Ann
Elizabeth
Binns
(1881-1950)

Arnold
(1872-1951)
m. 1906
Mary
Katherine
Harvey
(1876-1962)

Julia Seeboh
(1863-1869)

WHICH ROWNTREE ARE YOU?

When asked this question J. W.R. once replied 'The son of Drink and the brother of Poverty', his father having published a study of the drink problem and his brother Seebohm an important study of poverty in York.

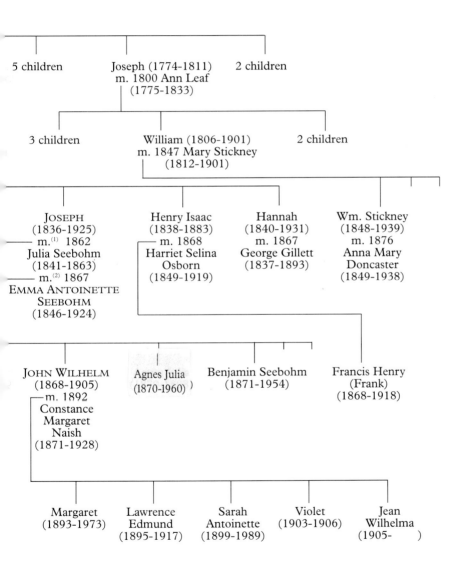

5 children   Joseph (1774-1811)   2 children
             m. 1800 Ann Leaf
             (1775-1833)

3 children   William (1806-1901)   2 children
             m. 1847 Mary Stickney
             (1812-1901)

JOSEPH	Henry Isaac	Hannah	Wm. Stickney
(1836-1925)	(1838-1883)	(1840-1931)	(1848-1939)
m.[(1)] 1862	m. 1868	m. 1867	m. 1876
Julia Seebohm	Harriet Selina	George Gillett	Anna Mary
(1841-1863)	Osborn	(1837-1893)	Doncaster
m.[(2)] 1867	(1849-1919)		(1849-1938)
EMMA ANTOINETTE			
SEEBOHM			
(1846-1924)			

JOHN WILHELM	Agnes Julia	Benjamin Seebohm	Francis Henry
(1868-1905)	(1870-1960))	(1871-1954)	(Frank)
m. 1892			(1868-1918)
Constance			
Margaret			
Naish			
(1871-1928)			

Margaret	Lawrence	Sarah	Violet	Jean
(1893-1973)	Edmund	Antoinette	(1903-1906)	Wilhelma
	(1895-1917)	(1899-1989)		(1905-)

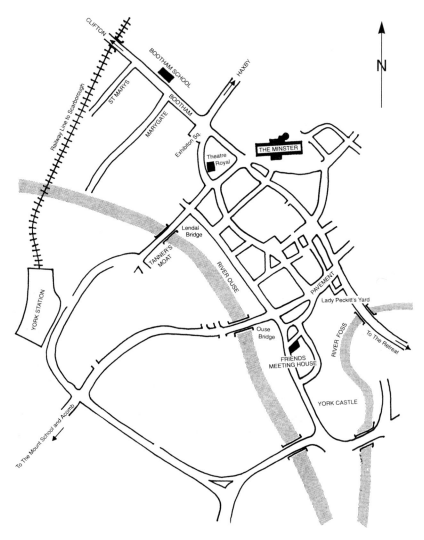

YORK (circa 1890)

Chronology

Foreword

by

Edwin B. Bronner

Emeritus Professor of History, Haverford College, Pennsylvania

JOHN WILHELM ROWNTREE first impressed himself on me 25 years ago while I was preparing to give the presidential address to the Friends Historical Society, delivered during London Yearly Meeting in 1970 at Exeter. That paper became part of *'The Other Branch,' London Yearly Meeting and the Hicksites, 1827-1912.*

Although I knew that John Wilhelm Rowntree and Rufus M. Jones had been great friends, and that they were buried side by side in the Haverford Meeting burial ground here in Pennsylvania,* I had not understood that he became a towering figure in London Yearly Meeting during his brief lifetime. Nor had I realised that he strongly influenced American Quakers during those years, both through his friendship with Rufus Jones and his work in England on the creation of Woodbrooke; also with his emphasis on intellectual growth and the spiritual ministry.

While reading Stephen Allott's splendid biography of Rowntree I realised that John Wilhelm's contributions to Quakerism all came during 12 short years, from 1893 when he spoke in London Yearly Meeting until his premature death in in 1905. In contrast, many of his friends lived to exercise great influence for a half century or more: Edward Grubb (1854-1939), John William Graham (1859-1932), and Joan Mary Fry (1862-1955), not to mention Rufus Jones himself (1863-1948).

John Wilhelm Rowntree exercised his influence through his personality, his speaking, and his published articles, including those found in *Present Day Papers*, which he edited. He did not publish a single book even though he envisioned several titles, including the scholarly series of Quaker history studies which were written by William Charles Braithwaite and

* see p. 136

Rufus Jones, with the assistance of others. The volumes are properly called the Rowntree Series.

While Rowntree looked with disfavour on the pastoral system, he did not reject pastoral Friends, and laboured valiantly to bring all the different Yearly Meetings together. He helped Rufus Jones to understand the importance of Quaker unity, and believed that Woodbrooke would serve as a place where all Friends might meet and learn to love and appreciate one another. Earlier he and George Cadbury had envisioned summer schools where Friends could gather to hear lectures, to study, and to enlighten themselves in a way which would strengthen the intellectual life of Friends and the ministry in Meetings for Worship. The summer school idea soon caught on in the United States, where sessions were scheduled, beginning at Haverford in 1900 with John Wilhelm Rowntree and William Charles Braithwaite participating.

Readers of this biography will enjoy all of it; for its portrayal of an outstanding Quaker leader, who was also a very human person and a family man deeply attached to his wife and children. The author has included John Wilhelm's delightful description of his travels in Palestine in 1895 in which his discussion of the various conflicting claims of religious leaders about the precise location of holy places is amusing as well as informative. He was most impressed with the beautiful mosque built on the site of the temple, the Dome on the Rock. He also visited the Friends school at Ramallah. Other examples of his writing are found in the appendices, ranging from inspirational essays to a recipe for making 1,200 pounds of 'Liquorice and Lemon Pastilles,' from his years in the factory.

Readers of this fine biography will be grateful to Stephen Allott for his research, writing style, and selection of materials to be included.

Haverford College   EDWIN B. BRONNER
Haverford, Pennsylvania
USA
January, 1994

Introduction

JOHN WILHELM ROWNTREE was hailed as a prophet by his contemporaries, and when he died tragically at the age of 36 many of the young Friends of his generation felt they had lost their leader. It was his plea in Yearly Meeting for tolerance of intellectual doubt which opened the way for the Manchester Conference, in which the Society of Friends for the first time faced the challenges of modern thought. The dogmas of fundamentalism had recently been accepted as essential to Quakerism in the Book of Discipline of London Yearly Meeting of 1883 and by American Friends in the Richmond Declaration of 1887. The powerful Home Mission Committee set up in 1894 made its chief work the preaching of this type of Quakerism in Meetings throughout the country, and the Society could well have developed on evangelical lines; but young Friends like John Wilhelm Rowntree and Edward Grubb found the denial of intellectual freedom intolerable. Some drifted away from the Society; others gladly accepted the new freedom which John Wilhelm had won for them and led the Society into the form of Quakerism which we know today.

The story of his life is, therefore, the story of how modern Quakerism came to be born as a faith based on experience. But it is also a story which challenges us with his belief that our meetings for worship need a vocal ministry enriched by a good religious education if they are to achieve spiritual depth, and it offers us the aim for Friends throughout the world of a reunion based on a faith in Jesus Christ which has faced all the doubts of modern thought.

John Wilhelm Rowntree was a many-sided human personality, generous and warm-hearted, sociable and witty, and yet knowing times of depression; he faced physical disability bravely and lived life to the full; he had a rich family life supported by a loving and very capable wife and was a successful business man; he loved people and they loved him. He was devoted to the Society of Friends and worked tirelessly for what he saw as its mission to the world. We are still enriched by what his life achieved.

CHAPTER I

Home and School

'WHAT SHALL WE DO ABOUT MOTHER?' was the agenda of a meeting of the children of Joseph and Antoinette Rowntree, called by their eldest son, John Wilhelm.

Antoinette was their father Joseph's second wife, the daughter of Wilhelm Seebohm of Hamburg; Joseph had met her in Hitchin in 1867 when she came to stay with relations to improve her English, and although she was not yet 21 years old, they were married within the year. Joseph's first wife, Julia, daughter of Benjamin Seebohm (who had settled in England), had tragically died in 1863, leaving a three-month-old daughter, so when Antoinette came to York four years later as a young bride she not only had to get to know the large Rowntree family of English relations, but had the care of a little girl, and a year later started her own family. So it is not surprising that there were strains for this young German wife and mother, which obviously her own family felt as they grew up, fond as they were of her. However the marriage was a successful one, for Joseph was an indulgent husband and together they delighted in their children of which there were six by 1884.

Their early education was given by a German governess who taught them German, and Antoinette shared her own interests in music and art with them. Joseph was not a strict Victorian father but treated his family with the same freedom as he had known as a child: they must have been a handful at times. Joseph and Antoinette lived at first in the house which his father had built for his retirement at the top of St Mary's; and since his death in 1859 his widow Sarah had continued to live there, but a separate front-door had been provided for the young couple's part of the house. Sarah was wise and understanding, and no doubt was helpful to her daughter-in-law.

Antoinette joined Friends soon after her marriage, but she never took the active part in the life of the Society which many of her Rowntree relations did, nor did she enter much into the society of the city. She must

1

Sarah Stephenson Rowntree 1806-1888,
mother of JR II

Julia Seebohm 1841-1863,
first wife of JR II

E. Antoinette Rowntree, second wife of
JR II, and John Wilhelm aged six and a
half months

have been very lonely and homesick at first, and anxious about her step-daughter, who died of scarlet fever in 1869 – her own first-born, John Wilhelm, then being only eight months old.

These were not easy years either for Joseph Rowntree. His brother, Henry Isaac, had bought the cocoa business from the Tukes in 1862, and in 1869 asked Joseph to join him from the family grocer shop in Pavement, where he gained his first business experience; he specialised in accounts, while H.I. supervised manufacture. The depression of 1873-79 made it hard for small businesses to survive, and when the death of Henry Isaac followed in 1883 leaving Joseph in sole charge, he was in a difficult situation, and sorely missed the companionship of his witty and light-hearted brother.

He had a lively mind, wide interests and a habit of researching thoroughly any subject in which he was interested, and his concern for the well-being of his work-people was linked to a general interest in social problems. As a young man he had gathered statistics on poverty, on which he had based his essays on 'British Civilisation' and 'Pauperism in England and Wales' (1865).

His father Joseph and his brother John Stephenson Rowntree had played a leading part in freeing the Society of Friends from its restrictive regulations on marriage and on dress. While he was a loyal Friend, his interests went far beyond the limits of the Society – John Bright who was disapproved of by conservative Friends for his 'creaturely activity' was one of his heroes. His home was therefore a stimulating one for children to grow up in.

Wider experience was also provided by holidays abroad. He had first gone to Switzerland with his solicitor cousin Joshua in 1864, and he travelled in North Germany with his first wife's father Benjamin Seebohm in 1872, while Antoinette, with the three-year-old John Wilhelm, visited her father Wilhelm in Hamburg. The years of depression curtailed travel, but in 1881 he accompanied Antoinette and the children to Germany, and also went with friends to Switzerland. After the death of his brother Henry Isaac in 1883 he took Antoinette and the three elder children to Switzerland for the first time, and the next year took John Wilhelm to Mürren: it then became his practice to take his children with him one by one to Switzerland, thus establishing a special link with each. The young John Wilhelm gloried in the grandeur of the mountains. (See Appendix A.)

In 1875, with three children now in the family, a larger house was needed, and the Rowntrees moved to No. 49 Bootham, now part of Bootham School; seven years later they moved again, to a house at the

3

bottom of St Mary's, which proved too small, and then back to the house next to where Sarah Rowntree still lived. When she died in 1888 Joseph succeeded to this house (known locally to the family as Top House, but later as Penn House, where they lived till 1905, and in time two sons and a nephew also made their homes close by in St Mary's, John Wilhelm occupying No. 30.

Like his father, John Wilhelm went to Bootham School (1880-86), though he also spent a period between 1883 and 1885 at the Quaker School at Oliver's Mount in Scarborough, probably in the hope that sea air would build up his health. His cousin Joshua saw him at meeting in Scarborough at this time and describes him as slight and delicate-looking: 'His deafness somewhat cut him off from boyish games. His mind grew all the more active in consequence. He was quick, curious and quizzical, with much fun and humour. He gave few outward manifestations of soul'. It is possible that he found life at school difficult. His deafness made it necessary for him to use an ear trumpet. This isolation, combined with a short temper and his dry sense of humour, may well have made him hard to get on with. Yet George Newman, two years his junior, remembered him as popular, both for his good nature and because of his disability. He began friendships at Bootham which were to be important in adult life.

He did not shine academically, although as an adult he clearly had the interests and abilities of a scholar. But school provided an intellectual stimulus which supplemented the talk at home on books and politics and art. He had a naturally enquiring mind, and there were lively minds on the Bootham staff to feed it. One of these, Benjamin B. le Tall, is described by Sidney K. Brown as 'the strangest mixture of literary and educational abilities', who was prepared to discuss any topic without reserve; 'his geography lessons were brilliant, he made history fascinating and early Quakers come alive by his racy style which still brought home his admiration for all they lived and died for'.

One of his masters wrote that Wilhelm was 'undoubtedly a boy of good natural ability, but being far from robust had never learned to use it effectively. He was not of a happy, contented disposition. He had not developed that genial brightness which was so striking when I have met him latterly'. Another master described how he coped with his deafness: 'he always sat by me to be able to hear, and when I had occasion to use the blackboard he followed me there. I always felt that he was a most appreciative pupil, anxious to learn and to miss nothing, and very grateful for any little one could do in helping him to take full advantage of his last year of school life.'

John Wilhelm and Seebohm Rowntree, c.1876

His sister Agnes, who was less than two years his junior, remembered him as a boy as

rather conspicuously straight and honourable with a delicate consideration for other people's feelings. He was *very* warm-hearted and always wanting to give people presents – he worried his mother by the amount he spent. An old house-maid who lived with us has written since his death, 'Master John was always such a little gentleman'. . . . He was by *no means* a saint when he was a boy. Seebohm [one year younger than Agnes] was always the good one and the peacemaker, while John and I fought. I think Seebohm and I rather feared his outbursts at one time – they were so violent. On one occasion (I think he was about 12 years old and at Bootham School) he bit a lady who was living with us at the time so badly on the arm that she bore the mark for years. I remember Seebohm and I narrowly escaped a chair hurled headlong across the room at us by dodging under the nursery table.

On the whole he was studious and interested in intellectual things rather than boisterous or wild. He was keen on natural history and collected butterflies and beetles. His command of language enabled him to upbraid us in no measured terms. His inventiveness was splendid for our games and he was the leader and originator of all the interesting ones. In early days in the nursery I remember his robber games when he built a robber den in a corner of the nursery, and we darted out in repeated sallies with booty stolen from the nurses – thimbles, cotton reels, hairbrushes, etc. – until they became absolutely frantic. I remember him roasting a wax doll of mine over the nursery fire, but as I never

John Wilhelm Rowntree, aged 16

6

cared much for dolls he was surprised when I became interested in the tragedy and joined in the sport.

One red letter day of mischief I shall never forget. The parents were away and Seebohm with them, and John and I were much vexed by the refusal of the cook (a very snappy person) to give us some implement which we needed, and we having decided her refusal had no justice in it, took steps for our revenge. First we played the garden hose into the kitchen window, and then on the window being closed, John crept into the back kitchen through a minute window, unlocked the door for me, when we both noiselessly arranged a pail of water where the cook would step into it. When she came in we proceeded to converse in loud tones about some fruit which we found cooling there – and which, I regret to say, we spoke of in such wise as to lead her to think we were mixing unholy ingredients with the prunes. Naturally this drew her and our scheme came off.

Joshua Rowntree quotes the comments of one who knew him well:

As a child, although very affectionate, he was of a passionate nature and he had to struggle against this weakness well into his school life. He was always truthful and honourable, but he had to fight against selfishness. He was a very close observer, was very imaginative, a great mimic and fond of acting. His deafness interfered with the enjoyment of school life, and probably was then acutely felt. A power of composition was early shown in childish harangues to his companions, and in essays contributed to the School Essay Society. (See Appendix A.) He had the artistic temperament strongly developed, with a great sense of beauty in nature and art. He showed

Agnes Julia Rowntree, 1870-1898

7

considerable facility in fine pen and ink work, and occasionally did a little oil painting.

He would have loved to be an actor, had it not been for this deafness. It is said that, as a schoolboy, he dressed up as a prospective parent and interviewed the headmistress of The Mount on the possibility of sending his daughter to the school – and got away with it. Agnes records that 'on his 21st birthday at a party in his honour he played Mephistopheles in some scenes from Faust. He got up the whole thing and coached everybody and painted scenery and was the life of the whole affair'. His strong imagination and his interest in people made him a good storyteller from the first.

Elfrida Vipont Foulds commented in her *Life of Arnold Rowntree* that Agnes and Seebohm were too young to recognise in John Wilhelm's tantrums the price which has to paid in childhood for the qualities of leadership, especially when frustrated by physical handicaps; they only knew that after the storm was over his warm-hearted generous nature reasserted itself and he was sorry for what he had done.

North Street/Tanner Row factory

8

CHAPTER II

The Cocoa Works

JOHN WILHELM left school in 1886 and started work in the Tanner's Moat factory, by the river just over Lendal Bridge. There were now over 200 employees. The death of Henry Isaac, his uncle, in 1883 had left his father Joseph in sole charge of the business. Times were hard, and in the first six months there was a loss of £385. But a new product, Gum Pastilles, had been introduced in 1881, and this may well have saved the business. Sales generally began to increase by 1886, so that John Wilhelm was joining a firm on its way to success: sales of £55,000 in 1883 had increased to over double by 1890, and were to reach £254,000 by 1897. Success was due in part to the improving economic situation, but also to the improvement of products. A Dutch type of cocoa, marketed as Rowntree's Elect Cocoa, was introduced in 1887, described as 'an extremely light powder, the essential product of the cocoa bean after it had been roasted and ground and the fat (cocoa butter) taken out by hydraulic pressure'. Joseph Rowntree was a good employer, and he knew how to delegate: he could convey his wishes clearly and in a few words – then he would leave the matter with the person concerned.

Young men of ability and drive, responded to this treatment. John was soon sharing responsibility with his father and became a partner at the age of 21. Way was thus prepared for younger members of the family to join the firm: Seebohm, who had been to Owens College, Manchester to study chemistry, came in three years after John, and their cousin Arnold Rowntree in 1892 (see Appendix D for a sidelight on their relationship at this time) and Henry Isaac's son Frank a year later. John specialised in the cocoa and chocolate departments, which he reorganised; he also overhauled both the office and the work of the travelling staff. As the business expanded larger premises were needed and development took place first on Wellington Row, next to Tanner's Moat, and then on the Haxby Road just outside the city boundary on the north side of the city. John threw himself into the planning of this with characteristic energy and worked out many of the details with great thoroughness.

Joseph Rowntree disliked advertising, especially if it seemed to make claims which could not be sustained – he felt that goods should be sold by their quality. Yet the young men realised that the advertising of their competitors would compel them to respond or go under. By 1897 big campaigns were being undertaken, as for example when free samples of Elect Cocoa were given away from special barges at the Oxford and Cambridge Boat Race.

John ('Mr John', to the work people) was remembered as a strict disciplinarian with a grasp of detail, who applied himself to business with extraordinary energy, sometimes overtaxing his physical strength so that he became overstrained and irritable; but he had also a charm of manner, kindliness of disposition and concern for the employees which won their respect and friendship.

He had taken part in the manual work of each department, learning the different processes by practical experience and taking careful notes. His first notebook, which is marked 'VERY PRIVATE', states that it contains 'notes taken at various times and in diverse manners in times past between the dates August 1886 and September 1887, and are not reliable for future work'. The neatness of the notebooks suggests that they were written up at leisure from rough notes taken earlier. The notes cover Gaget's Gum Department (Barker's, Henderson's and Padley's Divisions), Sydney's Cream and Chocolate Department, and Marriner's Department (with details, for example, of 15 recipes for different types of sweets and fruit jellies). Prices to wholesale houses were listed for 30 items in the Gum Department; also prices of utensils for different processes. There are tables of ingredients and notes on processes and equipment. Twenty-two varieties of chocolates made are listed and 14 varieties of creams. The last dated entry was made in '1st mo. 1888' (see Appendix B).

Later notebooks list 'private mixings' and 'private experiments', the dates being mainly between 1889 and 1895; towards the end of this period he must have sometimes used rough notes made by others, as work done while he was abroad in 1895 is recorded. The notes of 'mixings' detail different mixtures used, for example, for chocolate coverings. The experiments record trials of different mixings and processes, e.g. '1890 January 31 and February 3. A series of mixing was made, running down Exhibition Chocolate with the different butters, in order to test them against each'. Verdicts on the results are listed under the headings, Good, Better, Best, Not So Good, Vile (the last being reserved for Cadbury's butter!). A later series of butter cleaning received verdicts – and the comment 'Although Cadbury's Butter was better for filtering, it was Cadbury still and quite easy to detect'. Agreements to purchase some Fry's recipes for £5 each from S. Hewson were made during J.W.R.'s absence in Palestine, but he records the details carefully, including the arrangements for Hewson to come to York and make up the recipes and so prove they were the same as Fry's products.

The notebooks became more desultory after 1895, though he was still interested in experiments, as references in his journal of 1898 show (cf. Chapter X). But the business was expanding fast: there had been 200 employees in 1883, there were 893 by 1894 and 1613 in 1899. The firm became a limited liability company in 1897, and J.W.R. was made a director. But deteriorating health and increasing blindness were to enforce retirement from daily attendance at the factory in 1899, though he remained a director and took part in some of the firm's social activities. He was one of the first trustees of the three Trusts established by his father in 1904 to devote much of the wealth the business had created to wider usefulness.

CHAPTER III

The Adult School

'IT IS A GREAT BLESSING for a young fellow fresh from school to have the opportunity of meeting, week after week, with a number of men seeking to improve themselves mentally and spiritually.' So wrote his father in 1907, who had himself at the age of 21 taken on an adult class in the School in Lady Peckett's Yard, just behind the family's grocer shop in Pavement, and he had taken John with him as soon as he left Bootham. The class met on Sundays at 9.00 a.m. and John made his contribution from the start, lecturing to the Adult School monthly meeting on his experiences during holidays abroad; in December 1886 he spoke on the St Gothard tunnel and in September 1887 on climbing in the Alps (see Appendix C). This was the heyday of the York School – a record average attendance of 263 was reached in 1887 and the figure remained over 200 for the next six years. The decline thereafter was due in part at least to the removal of working people into the suburbs.

John, therefore, with his friend Edward Worsdell, opened a School in the suburb of Acomb in June 1893. It met at first in the tiny 15 ft by 22 ft Forresters Hall, and from November 1896 in specially built premises. Numbers rose gradually from six to over a hundred – the school appealing to thoughtful people, both committed Christians and non-believers. Joshua describes a typical lesson:

> He would begin with a hymn and a pause for silent prayer, explaining that he could not offer words as a formality to God. As time went on, he frequently did engage in vocal prayer. A portion of scripture read round by the men followed. The inner meaning of the passage was as likely as not to be a mystery to most of those who listened. Then, with clear, incisive sentences, the speaker would unfold some of the marvels of the universe. It might be the crust of the earth, or the stars, or some stirring life in the history of man. Whatever the theme, he won his audience by the wealth of

his knowledge and the generosity with which he presented it; and when their interest was aroused, and they felt they knew more on that particular subject than they had dreamed of before, he would bring all the light shed on the lesson round to the passage with which they had started, until it stood out with a meaning and a purpose quite new to those who listened. The closing hymn, men say, never sounded otherwise than genuine and appropriate.

His lessons were thoroughly prepared and he often had to rise early or sit up late to do the work he thought necessary, reading and preparing notes and diagrams. He liked to bring visual aids to illustrate his teaching of geology or of the history of the city.

He cared more [says Joshua] about drawing out than putting in. At the outset he would ask anyone who could not follow what he was saying to stop him at once. He welcomed interruptions gladly, and would at once turn to the blackboard or vary his illustrations to make things clear. He watched the faces of his class, and when once he felt sure he had them with him, it was not always easy to stop, but he insisted on some time for questions at the end, and in this he was rarely disappointed. His deafness was, of course, a difficulty, but to ensure everyone having a chance, the Secretary or someone who knew the men would sit beside him and make sure that no question was passed by; now and then he would promise to answer a question the next Sunday.

A scholar commented: 'We saw how he liked honest opinions from everybody, and how he wanted us all to think. He would teach more in a few words than some men could in a day'. As time went on Sunday School teachers and local preachers came to his class to get ideas (see Appendix E).

While numbers were building up, he made a point of visiting every member at home – a time-consuming process as he could not resist the invitation to a cup of tea; he visited the sick and liked to get to know everyone in the house. He entertained members in his own home once a week, and he held a reading circle, 20 to 30 gathering on Thursday evenings to read and discuss some serious book. He would follow up enquiries and lend books for further study.

There is no doubt that his own intellectual interests were fed and his education enriched by his Adult School work. Richard Westrope, who worked with him at Acomb, described how he 'gained a faith that was keyed to reason and to conscience and that covered all the facts of life. . . . He began where he was, and what he saw of the glory of science, the imperative of duty and the majesty of beauty he taught to others'. He

13

gained too a greater personal knowledge of working people and an understanding of social problems which were to become a dominant concern with him.

He came to feel that the Adult School meant more to him than Meeting for Worship, as he wrote to Fielden Thorpe, the retired headmaster of Bootham, in 1897. He had said the same at the Bedford Institute in May 1896:

> I believe it is often the experience of those scholars who come to our meetings, after previously attending their morning class, that they leave the meeting with the feeling that they had more real help in their school, that the teaching there was more direct, more practical, more powerful, more searching than the ministry in the meeting.

It was not surprising that few Adult School members became Friends.

The Adult School Movement had discovered a new method of evangelism, 'the method of Socrates and the message of Christ' – thought-provoking discussion and the family spirit of small gatherings, intensely human and open. This had been invaluable to those Friends who served it, liberating their energies and expanding their sympathies, but Friends did not see the opportunity for wider influence.

> Think [said John Wilhelm] how through them we might leaven public opinion, stem the forces of reaction, create a new and a tenderer conscience and a better love than the greed for gold, and might give to our country strong and God-fearing citizens who could bring Christian principle to bear upon public affairs! Think what outward results Christianity applied to our schools might achieve! Public houses and gambling dens replaced by lecture-halls and popular places of healthy amusement, slums abolished, and a healthy life made possible for the poorest!

He appealed to younger Friends especially to take a full share in the work. The gulf between Meeting House and Adult School needed to be bridged, and an equal effort made in the Meeting; for it would be suicidal to develop the Adult School at the cost of the parent Society itself.

The last years of his life saw a great extension of the Adult Schools in the suburbs of York and a growth in attendance from 362 in 1902 to 1,186 in 1905. Five new Friends' Meetings were started too: he could well have felt that the changes he had hoped and worked for were beginning to come about.

By this time he had become concerned for the Adult School Movement as a whole. He recognised the contribution of 'the cheerful sacrifice of scanty leisure by busy men' (like himself); they had solid gifts of experience of life, of human interest and concern, of open-hearted friendship, but they were poorly equipped for dealing with the intellectual problems 'concerning philosophy, biblical interpretation and scholarship, the psychology of the heart, and the ethics and economics of social life'. Special training was needed for at least a few who were naturally gifted, who could then in turn train the teachers. He made his own contribution in a history which he wrote of the Movement, in collaboration with Henry Binns, who did most of the research. It was published in Present Day Papers in 1902 (see Chapter XI), and then as a separate book (1903). This has recently been published, with a full introduction and additional notes, by Christopher Charlton (1985), as the first in a series in the Adult School History Project produced by Nottingham University Department of Education.

The development which was typical of many Adult Schools is illustrated in the History by an account of a 'a village institute connected with a northern Adult School' which in all probability was Acomb:

> It stands in the midst of a population of about two or three thousand, and was completed at the beginning of 1900 [the large hall built for Acomb Adult School was opened in November 1897, and extensive club premises added three or four years later], although some of the rooms had already been in use for three or four years. It now consists of a large hall capable of seating 400 persons, with a platform suitable for concerts and entertainments, a billiard-room with two full-size tables, a reading-room well supplied with papers and a good library, a small games room for pingpong etc., a bathroom with two gas-heated baths, and a women's room with a piano, used for the smaller meetings. The caretaker sells aerated waters and tobacco to the institute members. These number about a hundred from eighteen years of age upwards. The subscription is five shillings to men over twenty-one, four shillings to the younger members. During the winter months socials are held about once a fortnight for members and their friends; these attract many young people, and are under the supervision of the Vice-Presidents, who are teachers in the Adult School, and other members of the School and Institute Committees, some of these being women. . . . Cards are not allowed; and the large hall, which may be let for respectable entertainments, is only open after twelve o'clock by special permission of the President. . . . The members are practically all working-men. The number of young people who attend the socials of

15

this Institute is probably larger than in most Adult School Clubs; the right means of attracting this class has been carefully considered, and these socials have undoubtedly had a beneficial effect on the village life, and have widened the real influence and usefulness of the Institute. It is evident that young people of both sexes cannot find the same opportunities for wholesome social intercourse among the working-classes as among those who can boast more house-room; and we can hardly conceive of any social work of greater importance than the provision of such opportunities during winter evenings. The direct fruit of this work must be sought in the happier home-life of the village.

John Wilhelm saw the development of such social clubs as the means by which the Adult School Movement could serve society. The churches had little influence, religion being 'scouted by the majority as something unreal'. So 'let the Adult Schools cover the great cities with their parishes, establish their clubs in each inferno of grimed and sodden streets, and bring the witness of Christian fellowship to every home'. They were to be 'a true order of St Francis, fervent in spirit, serving the Lord'.

However the task was not merely social, to provide drink-free clubs, as Henry Isaac Rowntree had pioneered coffee-carts in the streets of York to offer an alternative to alcoholic drink. The religious need must be addressed, and especially in those schools which drew their members from among the better paid and better educated artisans. These were aware of some of the changes in religious thought of the past 50 years; they read free-thinking tracts; the intellectual questions must be faced with them, and new thinking about the Bible recognised.

This is what John Wilhelm was doing in his class at Acomb, but he saw possibilities which went far beyond that. He felt Adult Schools were to appeal to all classes, aristocrats as well as artisans:

> It is a want of imagination that confines the Adult School to a particular class. Discuss the deeper side of life at round table conferences – no priest, no parson, no holy order, simply human beings, laymen all or, as Friends say, Priests all in the sight of God.

Some schools did gather men of differing backgrounds: Edmund Harvey at Toynbee Hall in 1906 speaks of 'the wonderful way in which men of all class, from unskilled labourers to artisans, shopkeepers and professional men are brought together in truly friendly relationships, without sense of patronage'.

But good fellowship was not enough. He attacked the superficiality of the Pleasant Sunday Afternoon movement:

Everything, it is said, must be 'brief and bright'. The hour must not be exceeded. Solos, duets, recitations, freely interspersed with hymns, must occupy the major portion of the time. At all costs there must be no break or pause. The programme must be continuous as at a concert, lest the audience grow impatient. The address, often feebly humorous, and seldom profound, must be squeezed into twenty minutes, or, better still, a quarter-of-an-hour. The path to heaven must be pictured as though it wound always through flower-starred meadows under summer skies. A veil is drawn over the sterner truths of religion, and the solemn issues of life and death are but lightly handled.

He was equally scathing about the enthusiasm with which some Friends had been swept into the work of mission meetings:

The practice of worship amongst Friends in the early 60s . . . was largely unchanged; a somewhat formal conservatism prevailed. Into this atmosphere of suspended animation swept the hurricane of Moody's revival. Many Quakers were carried off their feet. For the first time in their lives they felt the uplift of congregational singing when the heart is in the voice. . . . When the hurricane passed, the landscape was changed. Crowds converted in the Mission Hall had found their way into the Meeting House. They were not prepared for the silence nor for a ministry of tangled texts set to a Gregorian chant. They chafed, hesitated, and slowly drifted away. But there were Friends, who, having laboured to draw them in, were not prepared to let them out! Adaptation became the watchword. There must be more freedom, there must be singing, there must be direct preaching. Step by step changes came, tardily at first, but, early in the 80s, with an increasing sweep. Admirable as was the spirit, there was, nevertheless, behind these changes a fatal misconception.

Such changes in America had led to the pastoral system, which John Wilhelm rejected. The alternative was an educated lay ministry, and it was to be his chief concern to work for this. In the Adult School the educational purpose remained dominant for him – he rejoiced when the last member of his class was converted to belief in evolution. Yet as the movement spread in York and new meetings were established in association with the Adult Schools of the suburbs, he came to wonder whether the overriding Christian purpose would not lead to some adaptation of Quaker ways. He ends his history:

Is it not possible that the Adult Schools are destined to modify or develop our ideas of church fellowship and of public worship? . . .

It is not desirable to found another sect, but it is surely desirable that those who have benefited at the hands of Friends, or of others, in the fellowship of the Adult class, should seek to make the union closer in the common bond of service and of love. . . . It may be the Adult School mission to promote a *rapprochement*, in which the churches, abandoning the straightness of tradition shall, in the liberty of the Spirit, accept a wider responsibility, and adapting themselves to changing needs, extend their fellowship and increase their power. . . . The idea of the Adult School, if it be faithfully realised, will prove a benediction, drowning the strife of cursing tongues, and healing, with the blessed peace of God, the ailment of Society. The war between capital and labour, the bitterness of selfish competition, the poverty that shames our land, the love-lessness of souls that know no Christ, call with one mighty voice for the labours of self-sacrificing love. May teachers and scholars share alike the mantle and the staff of this service, and build in their measure, and under God's redeeming power, the City of Happy Souls.

CHAPTER IV

Light and Darkness

THE LONG HOURS worked at the factory left little time for leisure, and the primitive conditions in unsuitable premises were exhausting: Seebohm later summed it up by saying, 'Tanner's Moat was Hell'. Work stopped at 2.00 p.m. on Saturdays, and Joseph Rowntree regularly took the train to Scarborough for a walk. No doubt his sons sometimes accompanied him; John's love of the North York Moors probably sprang from more than a year's schooling at Oliver's Mount.

Social occasions at home where guests were often entertained gave welcome variety, and John's wit and warmth blossomed on such occasions. As soon as he left school he joined the York Friends Literary and Debating Society, and for several years played an active part in organising events, speaking in debates (on top hats, for example, or women's suffrage, or taste and fashion, or railways and the environment) and after his marriage in 1892 he welcomed the Society to his own home. A prominent part was taken by Edward Grubb, even after he moved from York to Scarborough; other young Friends who occasionally lectured were John W. Graham, A. Neave Brayshaw and Edward Worsdell. Typical of the more ambitious events was the Conversazione held in the Exhibition Building on 16th April 1889: John was on the organising committee and booked the rooms; there were two concerts, a lecture on 'Treasures and Hearts' by J. W. Graham M.A., a magician and three tableaux vivants (did John take part in these? – he loved acting).

He visited London theatres during Yearly Meeting, to the horror of more conservative Friends. It is hard to believe that he did not patronise the Theatre Royal in York, perhaps with Seebohm. It was refurbished in 1888-89 and had an enterprising programme of visiting companies: Benson and Tree did Shakespeare; Pinero and Barrie were performed;

19

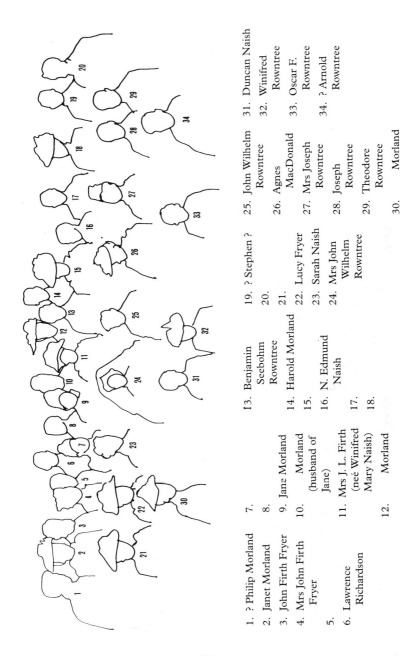

1. ? Philip Morland
2. Janet Morland
3. John Firth Fryer
4. Mrs John Firth Fryer
5.
6. Lawrence Richardson
7.
8.
9. Jane Morland
10. Morland (husband of Jane)
11. Mrs J. L. Firth (neé Winifred Mary Naish)
12. Morland
13. Benjamin Seebohm Rowntree
14. Harold Morland
15.
16. N. Edmund Naish
17.
18.
19. ? Stephen ?
20.
21.
22. Lucy Fryer
23. Sarah Naish
24. Mrs John Wilhelm Rowntree
25. John Wilhelm Rowntree
26. Agnes MacDonald
27. Mrs Joseph Rowntree
28. Joseph Rowntree
29. Theodore Rowntree
30. Morland
31. Duncan Naish
32. Winifred Rowntree
33. Oscar F. Rowntree
34. ? Arnold Rowntree

21

Irving and Granville Barker made guest appearances; there were regular pantomimes, and Carl Rosa and D'Oyly Carte put on opera.

There were socials too at the Meeting House – he mentions one which began with blind man's buff in the Meeting House Yard. Meeting provided the occasions when young Friends got to know each other. John is said to have met his future wife, Constance M. Naish, when she was a girl at The Mount, and he persuaded his sister to ask her home to lunch. Constance did not accept his first offer of marriage, despite her mother's warm encouragement, for she could have proceeded to college to pursue her studies in music or mathematics, but he persisted and they were married on 28th July 1892 – she was 21 and he 23; they set up house together at 30 St Mary's, just down the road from his parents. It was to be a radiantly happy marriage, blessed with five children – Margaret (1893), Lawrence (1895), Antoinette (1899), Violet (1903) and Jean Wilhelma (1905). Friends of all ranks and conditions were made welcome in the new home, and Constance gave John much-needed love and support in the trials which life was to bring him and in the wider work to which he gave himself unstintingly.

He had suffered since boyhood from deafness and even at school his sight was poor. Increasing blindness had been predicted in 1891, and three years later he was told on a visit to specialists that there could be no cure – he had in fact a life-threatening disease. Writing to his friend Lawrence Richardson in October 1894, he dismissed it in a sentence: 'My complaint is Retinitis pigmentosa, and Nettleship and Hutchinson have given me up.' However he found an American specialist whose strict regime limited the ravages of the disease for a time. He cannot have been a good patient – there was so much he wanted to do. Joshua comments: 'His endeavours to reconcile his passion for work with due obedience to his medical advisers often caused subdued amusement to his friends. He was ever ready to explain that a time of rest was coming speedily, when one or two things had been put right first.'

Later, when Rufus Jones had become his closest friend, he told him of the experience he had when the doctors dismissed his case, and Rufus recalled it after his death:

> Just as he was entering young manhood and was beginning to feel the dawning sense of a great mission before him, he discovered that he was slowly losing his sight. He was told that before middle life he would become totally blind. Dazed and overwhelmed he staggered from the doctor's office to the street and stood there in silence. Suddenly he felt the love of God wrap him about as though a visible presence enfolded him, and a joy filled him, such as he had

never known before. From that time . . . he was a gloriously joyous and happy man. His physical limitations have all along been turned into inward profit. His long, hard battle with a stubborn disease which was attacking the very citadel of his powers – his sight, his hearing and his memory – has only made him more heroic and gentle.

Friends have been meeting in Manchester since 1673 and on the same site since 1795. The present Meeting House, opened in 1830, was the venue for the historic Manchester Conference in 1895.

John Stephenson Rowntree, 1834-1907

24

CHAPTER V

Freedom to Doubt

T. EDMUND HARVEY, who was a boy at Bootham School from 1887 to
1891, later recalled seeing John Wilhelm sitting in Meeting beneath the
ministers' gallery, so that he could hear better what was said:

> We little knew then what was passing in his mind as we looked at
> his face, and may have even thought of him as somewhat tired of
> it all. . . . Yet all the while he must have been passing through that
> lonely spiritual struggle out of which he came forth with a keen
> desire to open his fellows' eyes to that Divine Light whose dawn
> he already saw. . . . What a debt we younger fellows felt we owed
> the man who dared to speak out for truth at all costs [he was seven
> years T.E.H.'s senior], for the honest statement of convictions and
> the honest refusal to repeat the words of the convictions of a former
> day, when they no longer bore the same meaning to us.

John described the period of doubt through which he had been passing in letters written to friends in 1893:

> I believe my spiritual growth . . . springs from the first doubt I ever
> felt, which was a doubt of the miracle of the raising of Lazarus. Till
> then I never thought, and I think I woke up simply to find that I
> had never really believed anything. I gave up one thing after another
> gradually, without any heart-rending or regret, I am afraid, but with
> sighs of relief, if anything – an unreality seemed removed when I
> had stripped myself of what in me it was mere cant to hold to, and
> it was as if I had cleared my mental decks for action.

> For two or three years I have been on the verge of resignation,
> and had it not been that I was favourably circumstanced, should
> no doubt have left Friends. How can we demand of the young

who are only on the threshold of experience an acceptance of dogmas the meaning of which they cannot fully grasp, and which experience alone can teach them to understand or value. To demand this is to create unreality in many at least, if not all, and tends I believe to check real spiritual growth. I feel for myself and for many other Friends that what we want is to strike a deeper note in our meetings for worship – deeper than the mere crust of words and almost of thoughts, to the living springs of actual spiritual experience.

I have known what it was almost to give up belief in God; I have certainly known what it is not to believe in God in my heart, but only with my head. I have known what it is to believe that there is no reality in the Bible – certainly no reality in Jesus Christ.

But by his middle twenties he could speak to the young men and women of his day with a fresh reality, could go with them into their own shadows of bewilderment and perplexity.

He published at this time a pamphlet on 'The Position of Young Friends in Relation to the Society', in which he admitted that many of his contemporaries were apathetic and worldly, yet they also had 'much earnest dissent from many commonly accepted dogmas'; he appealed, therefore, to both old and young, so long as they shared the root idea of 'the love and desire of God', to work together, 'however different the intellectual presentment of truth'. (See Appendix F.)

He got help in his own search especially from Richard Thomas of Baltimore, whose interpretation of Christianity, joining faith and knowledge together, was helpful to many young Friends. In writing later to his widow he recalled: 'He was to me a dear and intimate friend, and one who at a critical time in my own religious experience gave me, more than any one person I know, the help I needed.' It was an address of his, he said, that first enabled him to see Jesus Christ.

Richard Thomas was in fact present at London Yearly Meeting in 1893 when in the afternoon session of 25th May John Wilhelm made his plea for understanding of the position of young Friends. His words were to open up a new era in Quaker development. He spoke, he said, as one of the youngest in the Meeting (he was 24). He had enquired much among young Friends (*The Friend* reported) and found a large and growing section who felt their thoughts out of harmony with what they heard in meeting. They did not wish that those who were older should look upon them with suspicion and fear or think that they were trying to impress their views on the Society or to proselytise amongst those whose faith was firm. It was simply that they were not able to receive the truth themselves as it was uttered from the ministers' gallery; that it could only come to them, perhaps, by a life-long work. He had been pained to find out how this doubt – though there was true belief in it as well – was restrained from expression through fear of a want of sympathy from those who were older. He wanted that those who, like himself, were bound hand and foot, so that they could have no service in the meeting, would feel that their state was understood and regarded charitably and without fear. He thought that one cause of the existence of this negative principle in their lives was that the young man felt in meeting that he was out of touch spiritually with those about him, that he could not feel that there was a deeper unity in which they were all one. He believed that such would benefit a great deal from plain, uncontroversial sermons addressed to them upon the practical duties of life. Much that was spoken from the gallery passed by them and did not strike home; and if it was desired to strike home to them, they must be spoken to in their own language, the minister not yielding one iota of the faith which he held, yet speaking to them in the language which they understood. He hoped that by these words he had not pained those in the Meeting whose lives had a greater spiritual truth than his own. But he did desire that such as himself should not be looked upon by these with suspicion, but rather with a belief that those things in them which were of God would stand and that those that were not of God would not stand.

In the session which followed, William White (a national leader in the Adult School Movement) 'warmly sympathised', desiring that 'all the young men, of whom he knew many throughout the Society, would have their doubts solved in due time'. William Charles Braithwaite, who was six years John's senior, said that:

the stratum of members of whom John Wilhelm Rowntree had spoken claimed their thoughtful attention and loving interest. The Society was no longer secluded from the influences of the world about it; it was subject to the scientific spirit of the age. They could not be expected to look upon truth in the same way as their fore-fathers. These young Friends came to meeting week after week, earnestly desiring some message of spiritual life to their souls, and yet they might go away feeling that the meeting had been a burden rather than a help. The needs of the age might require, to some extent, a fresh costume for the form of truth which they desired to reveal, though the truth itself was the same – Christ Jesus, the same yesterday, today and for ever.

John left Yearly Meeting in a state of exhilaration, and wrote to a friend:

> We have spoken out plainly at last, and have been heard with wonderful charity and sympathy. There will now be no fear of a rupture I think, or need of aggressiveness, if only the spirit of the sittings is continued – while for those like myself it has been an immense stimulus for work. I don't see why, if a more earnest spirit is stirred up among our younger members, we should not fill the largest halls in a town; and I do believe ideal Quakerism is the religion for all who are drifting from orthodox nonconformity.

He was not the first to challenge evangelical orthodoxy. When later he was planning his history of Quakerism he headed a chapter 'The Rise of Modern Thought – the Lancashire Trouble'. He had traced 'the first valiant effort to break the crust of evangelical doctrine' to the group of Friends in Manchester led by David Duncan in the sixties. The Friends Institute had been founded there in 1858 'as a place where young men could get what was needful and useful without leading them into temptation' (they had been meeting in public houses for their discussions). By the early sixties 50-80 young men connected with Mount Street Meeting in Manchester were meeting in the Institute for lectures and discussion. Duncan lectured on *Essays and Reviews* (published in 1860 to advocate free inquiry in religious thought). He attacked the evangelical view of the Bible as 'fatal to all spiritual life'. In 1870 Yearly Meeting set up a committee to enquire into the division thus created in Mount Street Meeting; it set itself to root out the heresy. Eleven Friends resigned, and a separate Meeting for Worship was established. The movement died away, but the seed had been sown and support for new thinking began to grow. Henry Hipsley reacted caustically in Yearly Meeting in 1881: 'Young men who have doubts are made so much of, invited about and patted on the back as intellectually superior.' Rufus Jones however did not feel the affair worth mentioning when he came to write *Later Periods of Quakerism* which covers the 19th century.

In 1884 *A Reasonable Faith* was published anonymously to advocate experimental religion in place of dogma; it was vigorously condemned in Yearly Meeting in 1885, though the authors (who were well-known Friends) were able to defend their position. In 1886 John's close friend, Edward Worsdell, published *The Gospel of Divine Help*, a more scholarly exposition of liberal views: it received no notice in *The Friend* or *The British Friend*, and his views on the atonement caused him to be refused a post at Friends School, Lancaster (he had taught briefly at Bootham, 1880-81, resigning on health grounds); he later took a post at the Cocoa Works.

Edward Worsdell was concerned to face 'the difficulties supposed to attach especially to Christianity in view of the hypotheses of evolution and modern destructive criticism of the Old Testament'. Evolution, he maintained, was not inconsistent with moral conscience or with religion, but religious revelation could not contradict reason or conscience, which are God's gifts. He had come to believe that a loving God could not condemn to an eternity of suffering. In a footnote to the 2nd edition of 1888 he condemned the Richmond Declaration (see below) as a doctrinal statement which 'asserts explicitly all the characteristic and most objectionable dogmas of traditional theology', including eternal damnation. For him 'the great central fact was the eternal helpfulness of God'. He was resolved to 'run all risks and to follow only such teachings as his conscience would accept'. It was only little by little and through ten years of mental and spiritual conflict that he had come to see in the language of the New Testament unsuspected depths of spiritual meaning and constraining power and above all to see in Christ 'the Father of Lights' in whom is no darkness at all. In language which John Wilhelm was to echo he pleaded for the Society of Friends to gather to itself 'not only the poor and the ignorant but the intellectual also'.

In the autumn of 1887 evangelical Quakerism received its best-known expression at a conference of most American Yearly Meetings – the Richmond Declaration of Faith. But when it was put before London Yearly Meeting it was opposed, notably by William S. Lean, Thomas Hodgkin and John William Graham, who declared that the Friends who brought the document from the Richmond Conference 'had no idea that it would so deeply hurt the feeling of younger members'. Edward Grubb too spoke for young Friends: 'Do not seek to drive away such spiritual life as we may possess by presenting for our acceptance such a document as this.' It was not accepted, but was passed for printing in the Proceedings of Yearly Meeting.

John Wilhelm was not the first member of his family to see the need for change in the Society of Friends. He was said to be the inheritor in a large degree of the spirit of his grandfather, Joseph Rowntree (senior), who wrote to his son, John Stephenson, (21.4.1851) 'how few there are willing to give time, strength and property to the service of their fellow-creatures and to the affairs of our own religious body'. John Stephenson, in 1858, at the age of 24, wrote the prize-winning essay, 'Quakerism, Past and Present', on the causes for the decline of the Society; he urged the

Society to live for its mission, to give up disownment for marrying out and non-payment of tithes, and to consecrate itself for service by serious study. His own ministry appealed to the head as well as the heart; but he was concerned as to how John Wilhelm's campaign would develop. As his cousin Joshua remarked, it perturbed 'the watchman of his spiritual Zion, versed in the watchwords of a former generation'. But when it became clear that his nephew would not be 'merely critical but powerfully and vitally reconstructive, he rejoiced unreservedly, and between the two there came to be a strong bond of union in purpose and a whole-hearted sympathy'.

CHAPTER VI

Egypt and Palestine

March – May 1895

JOHN WILHELM had been initiated into foreign travel by his father and was keen to see as much as he could before his threatened blindness took effect. A visit to the lands of the Bible would also help his Adult School classes – he brought back numerous exhibits, including a mummy and 116 pill boxes of shells from the shores of the Sea of Galilee. He set off with Bedford Pierce, who had been appointed doctor in charge of The Retreat in October 1892, and was later joined by his old school friends, Lawrence and Gilbert Richardson of Newcastle.

He was clearly in high spirits, especially in the early stages of the journey. He gave each of his companions a nick-name in the journal which he kept: Dr Pierce was Herodotus, whose Histories contain the earliest tourist's account of the Middle East, Gilbert was Manetho, the Egyptian of the 3rd century B.C. who translated the records in the temples of Egypt, and Lawrence was The Philosopher, while he himself was Strabo, the voluminous Greek geographer.

Visits were paid on the way out to Rome and Pompeii, as he describes:

> At Rome Herodotus became strongly excited. Gulping down a cup of coffee he leapt with Strabo into a chariot and drove furiously through the Imperial streets. We stood on the floor of the Coliseum, magnificent beyond description in its solid and imposing ring of brick, rubble and stone. We photographed the forum, looked up at the Quirinal, saw the Arch of Constantine, the column of Trajan, peeped at the dome of St Peter's and in the space of one hour were back at our train. . . . Herodotus gloried in his attack of Americomania and seems to think one hour ample for Rome. The attack lasted all day and he has been boasting of his complaint to

an American doctor who looked at Herodotus with unfeigned envy.
. . . After Rome you will be prepared for the worst. We did Pompeii
in the afternoon. Naples we leave till tomorrow.

He was in fact greatly struck by the excavations at Pompeii and
commented, 'I think it would be worth while to travel from York to
Pompeii, see that and go back.' He also described with enthusiasm all he
saw in the streets, both in Rome and in Naples.

The streets may be dirty and the courts may be smelly, but the
street-scenes make up for everything. The small fiery horses (all
stallions here) which replace our broken-kneed cab-horses are gaily
decked out with tassels and wonderful metal ornaments kept bright
and polished. The nurses are more gorgeous than pen can describe,
entirely extinguishing an English alderman in his robes with their
wealth of colour, while the gendarmes are at any rate ornamental
corner pieces where the streets cross. All the women seem to have
good figures which they know how to set off to advantage, and I
was struck with the number of pretty (I don't mean beautiful) faces
in the passing crowds. It seems however to wear off fast, for the old
women are terrible hags.

They sailed from Naples on 24th March, reaching Ismailya through
the Suez Canal in four days. The first half of April was spent in a boat
trip up the Nile, with visits to Karnak, Abydos and Luxor and other sites.
By the 13th they were back in Cairo; here John Wilhelm was ill for a time
and missed some of the sight-seeing, but not the pyramids. He also went
to a boxing-match, after which he commented: 'I am inclined to think
boxing, without betting, should be taught at every Adult School.'

The landing at Jaffa, where they began their Palestine journey, is vividly
described:

There is no harbour at Jaffa, and when we came back on deck we
were quite at a loss to know where we were to land. There was the
coast; the houses of Jaffa, yellow in the sun, with white plastered
domes, seemed piled up one above the other as if scrambling out
of reach of the surf which came in white and angry. The sea was
grey and swelling in momentary mountains, that broke into foam,
and rushed past us with a grand sweep. The wretched steamer was
kicking and plunging like an impatient horse pawing to be off . . . .
I was wondering how we were going to get into the boats that were
closing in on us with their lusty shouting crews, when one of the
sailors began passing us down the landing steps at the side of the
steamer. All I remember was that I was told to sit down on the

bottom step. Below me, far out of reach, was the boat in a hollow of the surges – another instant, a wave lifted the boat to my very feet – strong arms picked me off the ladder, and the boat sank into the next hollow only to rise again.

Here they met the dragoman, John Harma, who was to take charge of the trip; he had previously escorted George Adam Smith round Palestine when he was writing his *Historical Geography of Palestine*, a real stroke of luck, as John Wilhelm had brought Smith's recently published book to serve as a guide. The journal continues:

> Jerusalem – On the first day, Friday, we drove with Harma our dragoman to the Mount of Olives. I write this account after four days' sightseeing, but I don't think there is anything I look back to with such pleasure as the Mount of Olives, even though it has not escaped the fate of everything here and is disfigured by churches and monasteries. If you wanted to convince anyone sceptical as to Christianity of the truth and beauty of its faith, the last place I would bring him to is Jerusalem. Here, if anywhere, I can fully forgive the scorn and contempt of the Moslem for the wrangling and squabbling sects which profess the Christ. One breathes freer in the Mosque of Omar than in the gaudy Christian churches.

He listed '17 superstitious sites' which Joshua Rowntree omitted when he edited the text!

> Of course as regards sites, there is little or no certainty, and an enormous amount of superstition and tradition. But the more one sees the lie of the land, and learns the connection of things and to *know* Jerusalem, the more one feels that there could be no other Mount of Olives. It is so pre-eminent, the view is so much the finest and the position fits in with the Bible narratives. I think I am inclined to pin my faith to the Mount of Olives. But not – emphatically not – to the Garden of Gethsemane. . . . The path round the garden is marked off every few feet with a gaudy picture of a shrine. Once in, you are shown where Peter slept, James slept and John slept, where Judas stood when he kissed Jesus, etc. – as if someone went round with stakes to mark the different places at the time. Close by is a hideous Russian church. It is a relief to pass on through wheat fields, and pass the olive, almond and fig trees which dot the slopes, picking the brilliant poppies as we climb, and turning now and then to look at the extending view. Two other churches spoil the summit; they stand some distance apart, but both mark the exact spot where Christ ascended to heaven.

The Temple Area – Saturday April 27th. The morning was well spent. It was a relief to be among Mohammedans again, and I must say I am glad the Temple grounds are in their hands. We went straight to the Haram es Sherif, the great enclosed area where the Temple once stood, and where now is the beautiful Mosque of Omar. We had to have an escort of two soldiers, and a permit from the British Consul, and felt quite important. . . . We pick our way through various Mostabas, raised places where Moslems pray in the open air, and then ascend a broad flight of shallow steps, and, passing under a ruined arcade with graceful pillars, we find ourselves on the highest plateau, on which the Mosque itself, the Dome of the Rock, stands. Here no doubt was the Temple, and the Mosque may very possibly cover the site of the Holy of Holies. . . . This world-famous building is, in its particular way, the most beautiful I have ever seen. The exterior decoration is wonderfully intricate, and here and there the design is extremely beautiful. Blue and white predominate, especially the former, and a good deal of yellow comes into the composition also. . . . Each tile is separately burnt with a separate design; many are Persian, and some of the richest effects are produced by blocks of coloured glass set in cement. With strong sunlight upon it the effect is wonderful. . . . Round the centre space runs a wrought iron screen, and in the centre lies a naked rock. . . . The Moslems claim that it is the centre of the world, that God will sit on it on the Judgement day; that it is poised on air, and though apparently resting on a wall below, is not really resting upon it, only pretending to. Mohammed sprang from this rock to go to heaven; you are shown where his head broke through the roof, so it must be true; and the rock was so anxious to follow that the angel Gabriel had to come and hold it down. You can see his finger-marks, so that must be true also.

Sunday April 28th. We walked down into the valley of Kidron, and examined what is called Solomon's quarry. . . . Opposite is one of the suggested sites for Calvary – much more to my mind than any other I have seen. It is a low eminence overlooking the road, and with caves in its rocky face. But of course it is the merest surmise, and I don't quite see how the real site can be found. Neither do I see why it matters, or what good would be done if it was found. The flame of superstition would have added fuel to feed it, that is all; and a great deal of sentimental writing would be produced by as many future Cook's tourists. I prefer the present doubt. . . .

Equally sceptical were we at the convent which contains the ruins of the Roman Praetorium and the site of the judgement of Christ. But we enjoyed this visit. We were taken round by a dear old nun, with the face of angel, and the grace and manners of a high-born lady. There was an indescribable flavour of sweet cloister piety about everything, and everything was beautifully fresh and clean. We felt as if in a Friends' Meeting-house in the neat, simple room. . . .

Bethlehem – We sketched the view from Bethlehem after enduring the incense and candles for a while, and walked back in the sunset light. Only then did the full glories of the Holy City appear, as we approached along the broad carriage road from Hebron, the mountains growing violet in shadow to the east, while yet a liquid yellow light lit up the city walls. The sense of the past history is choked out in these chapels, but out in the open you breath freely, and catch something of the inspiration of the place. The Galilean in His rough peasant dress and turban, no doubt, had wandered in the evening over these hills with His rude following of fisher-folk, every whit as humble and obscure as the peasant we met on our way. To those who believe that Jesus was born in Bethlehem the Church of the Nativity may appear to occupy the real site.

Camp Life – The life in camp is very healthy and really very luxurious. We two Englishmen have no less than eight servants and eleven four-footed beats and three tents! It is a picturesque sight to see the camp following sitting round, Eastern fashion, eating out of the common flesh-pot, the red glow of the charcoal and the faint glimmer of the lamp flickering on the dusky limbs and many-coloured raiment. That is the sentimental hour, when, the heat of the day forgotten, and the glaring hills softened to mysterious violet in the gloom, we stroll, with cigarettes lighted after the sumptuous evening meal, up and down our temporary 'Castle'. Then tongues are loosened and there steals a comfortable sense upon one of being at peace with all the world. We accept our dragoman's invitation, and squatting down Arab fashion among our cooks and muleteers, drink the coffee of friendship with them. Then come the jokes at our remissness in rising, how often we had to be called, and the time we take to dress, and the things we leave in the tent; or we praise our cook's soup and his excellent rice pudding and his vegetables and chicken; and after more amicable converse and tales of former adventures with other parties from the valiant John (the dragoman), we turn in

35

under the brilliant stars and the waxing moon to sleep the sleep of the just.

Near Jericho – It was really a cool day for the Jordan valley, though it was 100°F in the shade. . . . We reach at 12, after four hours riding, the 'Apostles Well', another merely traditional name. Round this is gathered a concourse of Bedanese, donkeys, women, children, horses and fine dark-looking men, in black and yellow striped cloaks and black kuffiyehs, armed with a short knife and gun. They are of particular interest when one remembers that they give us a picture of what those wandering Hebrew tribes, under their great powerful sheik Moses must have looked like, when they came as invaders to the land of the Canaanite – a great wave of emigration out of the desert sea away there behind Moab. One feels grateful for the realistic picture of the past which such a scene affords. I watched these people giving their beasts the longed-for draught, as we sat at our lunch, and felt that the Old Testament was getting to be real for me bit by bit, though one's western ideas need considerable re-adjustment at first. And if it is reality from which much that we call 'miraculous' had to be eliminated, this elimination is not a loss, but an infinite gain. The unbridged gulf that yawns between a past teeming with miraculous interventions, and a prosaic present where miracle is reduced to law, is bridged by a new human interest, as one *feels* old Bible people were only human beings after all, and subject to the same unalterable laws of God, the same yesterday, today and for ever.

Ramallah – Our detour to Ramallah proved interesting. The American Friends have a mission here, which we visited. It is chiefly for girls, who live partly as boarders – I think 24 reside on the premises – the rest in the village. Ramallah is decidedly cleaner than most of the villages. It has several missions, which seem to be doing their duty socially as well as religiously, and bringing about a better sanitary condition. I noticed the bright faces of the women. . . . The girls sang hymns to us in English and Arabic, in a schoolroom filled with European furniture. I only objected to their costume, sober and Quakerly perhaps, but a prim uniform, most incongruous and unsuited when you have the Oriental sense of colour to guide you. Leave the national dress alone, I say.

Samaria – Crossing the well-cultivated fields and picking our way up through a large fig orchard, and then through ripening corn and banks of glorious flowers, morning glory, dahlias and pinks, etc., we find ourselves at an olive tree, large and isolated at the entrance to a shallow wady, standing alone on the height with ruined masonry under its shadow. Here we spread our carpet and lunch. The spot is now called Seilun; once it was Shiloh, to which memories of the Ark of Eli and Samuel attach themselves. Now there is nothing for the eye to rest upon except open vales of ploughed land and corn – rounded hills of undecided outline. Bees are humming and passing from flower to flower, beetles swarm, flying with heavy clumsy flight across the field, and everywhere the nimble lizards pop in and out among the stones. A gentle sea breeze tempers the noonday heat. . . . On our left, immediately facing us, Ebal and Gerizim, reminding me forcibly of the Malvern hills. At our feet the long fertile upland plain of El Muknah, and beyond over a distant ridge of mountain, faint, indescribably delicate with its fairy-like blue and white, the splendid triple crown of snowy Hermon. . . . We struck off early to the right to climb Mount Ebal, leaving our horses in a cemetery. . . . We had a perfect day and a marvellous view. I have never had the sense of looking down on so much outspread history before, and over such a vast extent of country. Our northern limit was Lebanon – 150 miles away, to the south the upland of Judea beyond Hebron, fully 50 miles away. To the west there was the sea, to the east we saw beyond Galilee, beyond Jordan, to the mountains of the Hannam. It is not often given to mortal men to scan at a glance 200 miles of country, where almost every peak suggests or conceals some historic spot. I gave time to sketching a complete panorama, which I managed to secure in spite of a blazing sun, from which no protection was possible, and the fact that it was not possible to get the view from one spot. . . .

Coming down we ride through the whitewashed town and lunch in an olive grove which overlooks the valley. I must say that while Nablus looks beautiful from below or on the approach by road, the view down from where we lunched or from Ebal is the reverse of pleasing – the flat roofs look so unprepossessing as you see them from above. . . . Illustrative of the happy-go-lucky character of Oriental sanitation I may here record *en passant* that barely outside the town, on the Tafa highroad, one of the few real roads in Palestine, we passed a dead donkey decaying with intolerable stench, one leg already a bleaching bone and two men cutting off what was no doubt their supper from its corrupting sides. Excuse me, but a detail like this is necessary if you are to understand the difference between East and West! . . .

Down into a lovely glen of olives and figs, past a well where the women were gathering for water, and up a stony steep path to a platform brought us to Seboste. This miserable village – all that is left of the city of Omri, of Ahab, of Herod, crowns a hill surrounded on all sides by fertile valleys. . . . We pitched on a platform which was levelled to make a site for a temple of the Herods, and indeed the hill is everywhere terraced, and ruins peep out of a tangle of weeds and towering thistles. I don't think we have before or since had the impression of decay and of the glory of a departed civilisation so strongly as at Seboste, with its ruined theatres, its desolate colonnades, its ruined wheat-sown hippodrome, cut in a huge semi-circle into the hill-side. This little wretched village does not suggest a siege by Ben Haddan, or a three years' struggle with Sargon. Where is all the Greek and Roman life that once made the hippodrome, the theatre and the temple gay with the colour and the movement of many people? What tales of passion, love, hatred, slander, of devotion and of selfishness lie buried under the wheat-fields? What a contrast, these ragged tatterdemalion peasants, droning out a monotonous and unintellectual existence, year after year following each other with Oriental sameness! . . .

With all their poverty and rags I have not seen what I call really degraded looking people, unless the Jericho Bedouins can be called so. Certainly you do not see, either here or in Egypt, in a whole tour of months, such as I am taking, as much real degradation, as much selfconscious degradation, as you can see in the low parts of London in one day. Here the most ragged beggar has some suggestion, at any rate, of dignity about him.

We ride all day through a succession of broad, flat bottomed valleys – which seem to be the feature of Samaria as the upland downs are of Judea. . . . The reapers are at work in the barley fields, the vales being alive with peasants for the first time. The women reap in long rows, squatting on their heels, with their skirts tucked up to the waist, singing as they reap with primitive hooks. Those who have babies bring them along in sledges covered with filthy cloth hangings. Every now and then a little naked fly-pestered thing is taken out to be fed. We pass a well where there is the usual pretty group of women, in this part of the country remarkably beautiful and attractive, and quite conscious of the flashing brilliance of their teeth, as they smile at you. The well-side in Palestine takes the place of the afternoon tea-table at home. It is here that the gossip and the scandal take unto themselves the swift wings of speech, while at home it is whispered over the tea and biscuits, with chairs drawn close and many an expressive look! . . .

Road across level plain, ploughed land and cornfields, to Mount Gilboa, starting at 8.00 a.m. Reached the summit of this bare rocky hill by 10.30, to find a dirty village occupying the best point of view, with a cactus hedge doing its best to obstruct where possible. Here was a woman wielding a distaff, and from awful holes in the ground crept out numerous dirty children, dogs and chickens, which apparently live together. In spite of the dirt, the girls here too are very pretty. . . . I gave my strength, however, not to the villagers, but to a careful sketch of the views, which took some considerable time. I wanted to get a thorough grip of the plain of Esdraelon, and the subsidiary plain of Jezreel, with a view to a better understanding of their bearing on history. . . . [At Megiddo] I sat on the roof of one of the dwellings, and looking across the thistles and the great sheets of ripening corn, took a pencil sketch of the historic pass, by which so many armies have tramped north or south, to or from the Vale of Sharon. . . .

Nazareth – A first view of Nazareth is most disappointing. Hideous modern churches and an excessively vulgar renaissance residence or school, brand new, are the objects which strike you as you breast the rise in the road and ride down through the suburbs. We pass the well, the *only* spring, where, no doubt, young Mary came with the other village girls to gossip and perhaps get impatient for her turn as the girls do now. They were laughing and chatting, and I am afraid pushing and squabbling, as no doubt in days of yore, a gay motley crew in their loose, baggy, many coloured trousers and sashes. We made up our minds we would keep to the hills, do no sightseeing, visit the well once or twice and stop two days. This we did, and as a consequence Nazareth grew upon us. We have not had our memory marred by monkish superstition, candles, incense and false relics and sites. We carry away with us chiefly the memory of breezy hills with an extensive prospect, of a grey-green hollow dotted with white houses and a few cypresses, and perhaps above all the gay bustling scenes around the village spring. . .

I wish, as over and over again I have wished while in Syria, that I could number botany as an accomplishment. I can only say of the Nazarene flowers that the ground seemed mainly covered by a sort or scrub – not prepossessing – which is enlivened by pinks, purple asters and the same hollyhock-like plant I noticed in Carmel.

The Lake of Galilee – the ride down was not eventful, nor was it at all a striking one. . . . Great herds of black cattle, driven by Bedouin with formidable clubs and staves, passed us from time to time. We purchased specimens from the astonished natives to illustrate the rod and staff that comforted freebooting David, who must have been far more like the fierce dark-looking cattle drovers in their black and yellow cloaks than the idealistic pictures one is accustomed to.

At last the lake of Galilee comes into sight. The long level wall of the opposite shores – unrelieved and unbroken – the one relieving feature, Old Hermon, presiding over the scene at the northern end. Nothing has surprised me more than Galilee. I suppose one unconsciously idealises historic scenes such as crowd the shores of this lake, and it is somewhat disturbing to preconceived ideas to find these stirring scenes set in such commonplace surroundings. But the dreariness of Galilee is not its worst feature – the dull basalt shores are at least more tolerable than the awful oppressiveness of the climate.

Our descent was steep, and our first view of the one town, Tiberias, striking and picturesque. . . . We rode through its close stuffy streets, hung across with rags to keep off the sun; we looked into its slummy courts, smelt its many and fearful smells and were not surprised to see the washed-out pale faces of the inhabitants. . . . At night the temperature fell to 75°F. It was not possible to sleep much – the dense swarms of mosquitoes defied evasion and got inside the curtains. The poor camp followers had a fearful time of it – John being bitten all over his portly self and very doleful thereat in the morning. In addition one of the grooms caught a fever, small wonder – and we were glad when, on 16th May, we set off over the hills to Huleh, a doleful and washed out crew.

The Galilean Hills – At a spring and beside running water we lunched. An old mill stood near, and here evidently the cattle from far and near were wont to take their noonday siesta. It was not long before we were surrounded by a lowing herd, and finally we found our operation with the sardines and soda water followed in breathless suspense, awe-struck and admiring, by 13 Bedouin shepherds. One of these was playing a lute made from a reed, and carved rudely during his leisure hours. Being again reminded of David, I managed with some diplomacy on John's part to purchase this treasure for the vast sum of threepence, which seemed mightily to please. . . .

When we went to bed there rose on every side, not a murmur, but a roar of frogs – even I could hear it. Again the temperature fell only to 75°F and again the close, damp air made us suffer considerably. I had just dozed off when a crash woke me. The Philosopher was lighting the candle, and the tent was every now and then lit up by vivid flashes of lightning. The rain was coming down in torrents and the wind, blowing a hurricane, had almost carried off the tent. Found Strabo and the Philosopher sitting up in bed, luggage scattering over the marsh, and the tent no one knows where. However John was out before we had time to call, and we heard him and his men rush out into the rain and hold on to the straining ropes, hammering down the pegs and making all square again. It was a near shave, but soon the storm rolled away down into Galilee, muttering and rumbling among the hills, and we were able to turn over and sleep with our confidence in our dragoman considerably increased. . . .

Starting before eight, we rode weary and unrefreshed by our sleep over the steaming plain – all of the streams swollen with muddy torrents from the rain, and the ground soft and muddy. It was squelch, squelch through the bog, and splash, splash through a running stream, or stumble, stumble over rough, rocky paths – and all the while you were steaming in a Turkish bath. At seven o'clock breakfast the thermometer has risen to over 80°F and was rising then, and a damp heat like that is as exhausting as anything I know. We were scarcely in the mood to enjoy the glorious banks of oleander or wonder at the great masses of papyrus. But at length the change came. We crossed the plain to the east and breasted the first low spurs of Hermon; we had crossed the Hasbana, one of the sources of Jordan, a cold mountain stream roaring down over its rocks like a Swiss torrent, a most welcome sight and carrying with it a whiff of the pure mountain air. We had lunched under fig trees within earshot of the roar of Jordan's main stream issuing from its cave, and were close under the fine castled hill of Banias, the ancient Caesarea Philippi, when lo! behold the clouds vanished and from the west, chasing them before him, came the cool sea breeze. . . .

And so we passed out of Palestine, zigzagging up, up in magnificent air, and with widening views over the Galilean hills – up till the valleys became rocky and bare, and the snow on Hermon seemed

41

close too. Half-an-hour's climb above, and finally breasting a ridge of rock we came on a mountain valley under Hermon's very crown, and there were our tents pitched by the village of Mejdel esh Shems, between 3,000 and 4,000 feet *above* the sea. The air was magnificent, and we noticed at once the difference in the people. Down in Galilee and Huleh they were a poor, fever-stricken set of people with no go about them; here the children were romping about the green, the men were fine and sturdy, and the women good-looking and with plenty of colour in their cheeks. We went to bed with all our available rugs, etc. pressed into service, and a hot water bottle was actually a comfort. Temperature at night 47°F.

Lawrence Richardson later commented on his experience on this journey:

It has been my good fortune to travel abroad with John over a total distance considerably more than the circumference of the earth, and all who knew him well understand the privilege it was. He was so keenly interested in everything and had always taken such trouble to find out and read up the best books on the countries visited. In Palestine he read aloud George Adam Smith's *Geography of the Holy Land*, a book which shows how the physical features of the country affected its history and thus doubles the interest of seeing it. John was very fond of reading aloud on his journeys, either some descriptive book like that just mentioned or, in idler moments, some well chosen novel. He could undergo considerable fatigue, though rather easily upset by changes of temperature or diet, but he had a remarkable power of recovery. His helplessness in strange places in requiring someone to lead him wherever he wished to go must have been a severe trial, but he rarely showed that it was so.

Postscript: The Amateur Photographer – At Naples I had with me a companion both charming and witty. He had only one fault: he was an amateur photographer. Perhaps I must not blame him. In these days . . . we trace everything to heredity. We don't blame, we never get angry, we only murmur 'poor fellow', and sincerely pity.

It was lovely weather. We had knocked off Rome in the early morning. Not built in a day, they say, but it had revealed its charms to us in an hour, and in the afternoon we were on the threshold of the City of the Dead. Still in the narrow, untenanted streets you may trace the ruts of the chariot wheels, and picture to yourself what grand old rows there must have been between the Pompeian cabbies as to right of way. . . . But the quaint little wine and oil shops, with their marble slabs pierced with round holes for the cool stone jars, the mosaic shop signs, the shocking depravity of brick fluted columns covered with cement – shams even in ancient Pompeii – the real lead pipes in the baths . . . all these wonders fished out of the lava deeps were only so much stock in trade for my friend the amateur. . . . For the whole of a long afternoon our amateur toiled on. He was very diligent. He climbed up impossible ways, up dangerous crumbling walls and fixed his little instrument with skill, first for this and then that panorama. He was very careful. How he calculated the time exposure in all the difficult circumstances, how he watched the direction of the sunlight, how he sought for fine effects of light and shade. . . . And when at last we found ourselves in the train, coasting the bay, and nearing the twinkling lights of Naples, it was not to be wondered at that I was treated to a retrospect of the labours by which

an amateur became a master. Solemnly was I warned of the pitfalls besetting' the unwary footsteps of the tyro. I was properly humbled, both at the magnitude of the enterprise if I aspired thereto, and the height of the pinnacle from which my friend looked down.

It was somewhat unfortunate, indeed *very* unfortunate, that on arriving at the hotel, our friend the amateur found he had made a little omission. He had, in fact, forgotten to put any films into his camera, and I am given to understand that without films photographs are apt to be obscure.

Arnold Stephenson Rowntree 1872-1951
son of John Stephenson Rowntree 1872-1951
Liberal MP for York

CHAPTER VII

On to Manchester

'ON THE WHOLE,' John wrote in June (1893) 'Yearly Meeting has stimulated me. I see more what is wanted, and I feel more determined than ever to devote my life to making the Society of Friends, as far as my little power and little scope allow, a real and living force in the world.' He wrote a pamphlet, which was published in July, on 'The position of young Friends in relation to the Society', expanding on what he had said in Yearly Meeting and appealing for 'both old and young to see the possibility, so long as the root idea of the love and desire for God be the same, of working together, however different the intellectual presentment of truth'. (See Appendix F.) This produced a large correspondence; he was in demand as a speaker at meetings and gave papers on 'The Future of Quakerism', 'War', and 'Science and Religion'. He was amazed at the prevailing satisfaction with the status quo and was determined not to 'sit still and do nothing'. Edward Grubb, who also accompanied him on his visits to other meetings, addressed a special meeting of 170 young Friends held at Yorkshire Q.M. in 1894 on 'The responsibilities of the rising generation in relation to the Society', and John himself, according to the account in *The British Friend*, 'gave an earnest address, expressing dissatisfaction with the present condition of the Society of Friends; if Young Friends would only rouse themselves, he felt sure there was a great work for them to do; in the world at large there was a social and religious upheaval; now was the time to show the true principles of Quakerism in response to the call for less formalism and more reality; our strength would lie, not so much in unity of thought, as in unity of aim.' He was described later by Harold Morland as the spiritual father of the Young Friends movement.

In Yearly Meeting 1894 he again spoke on the state of the Society:

> . . . the common foe [he said] was not difference of thought but indifference; we could meet together in practical work even while

44

we thought differently; if there could be a freer atmosphere in our meeting houses with real love and practical sympathy expressed for those who differed in thought, we should go forward with greater power; in the belief in the acknowledged guidance of God in the heart there was enough unity for any church to base itself upon.

The same Yearly Meeting set up a Home Mission Committee of about 80 Friends appointed by Quarterly Meetings to further outreach or extension in any form. It encouraged local evangelistic work through the appointment of paid mission workers. But it also included a number of liberal younger Friends who persuaded the committee to suggest to Yearly Meeting a conference to be held in Manchester in November 1895 'to consider how the spiritual and historical heritage of the Society could be revitalised by facing the discoveries and perplexities of the real contemporary world with an enthusiastic Christian faith and ministry'. John was not himself a member of the Committee, but his cousin Joshua Rowntree and his uncle John Stephenson Rowntree were, and Joshua became chairman of its executive committee and of its conference sub-committee.

Yearly Meeting agreed and in November over 1,000 Friends met in Manchester for three days to listen to more than 30 papers, mainly of a liberal trend. It was the first time the Society had been able to assess its position in the light of modern thought (more than 30 years after the publication of Darwin's *Origin of Species*). But it was too soon for open and free discussion. In the session on 'The Society of Friends and Modern Thought' the case was made for fearless study of the Bible, and Sylvanus Thompson, a leading scientist, declared his sense of spiritual security in being at once a Christian, a Quaker and a scientist; the meeting agreed that there should be no discussion, after some Friends made it clear that they could not agree with what had been said.

John Stephenson Rowntree presided at the first session and gave a paper on Early Quakerism. In the afternoon of the first day John Wilhelm gave one of the five papers on the message of Quakerism to the world (see Appendix G) and Edward Worsdell supported him in the discussion. The aim of the conference was not only to make known the distinctive views of Friends, but to consider the needs of thoughtful and educated young people in the Society, and this theme was often mentioned. Hannah Doncaster prefaced her talk on social questions with a description of the situation of such a young Friend, who could well have been John Wilhelm himself (see Appendix H). Young Friends also spoke in the sessions and referred to his paper.

The coming development of his concerns was fore-shadowed in George Cadbury's plea for an educated ministry to help in the spreading of Friends Meetings, and also in Joseph Rowntree's paper which included the suggestion of a centre or settlement where young men and women could gather round a gifted teacher and, 'through personal association and the influence of spirit upon spirit and wise guidance and instruction' as well as practical work in the neighbourhood, be fitted for service in our Meetings in teaching or ministry.

Joseph Rowntree II, 1868
the year he joined H. J. R.

CHAPTER VIII

Rufus

RUFUS JONES was a leading American Quaker scholar, who travelled widely among American Yearly Meetings and in 1894 had become editor of *The American Friend*, concerned for the drawing together of separated American Friends. In 1896 his board encouraged him to gain more experience of English Friends. He attended London Yearly Meeting and visited Friends in the north of England. John Wilhelm was at Yearly Meeting also, but they may not have met till the following year when Rufus went on a walking holiday in Switzerland with Rendel Harris (an old friend, as he had taught for six years at Haverford where Rufus was a student). His description of their meeting forms the climax of the second volume of his autobiography, *The Trail of Life in College*:

> We both knew that a group of English Friends, including John Wilhelm Rowntree of York, were having their holiday in Mürren and we measured off our day's marches so as to arrive there for a week-end. It proved to be one of the most eventful and important week-ends of my life. At a little Quaker meeting which we arranged in the Hotel Mürren for Sunday morning Rendel Harris quoted Christina Rossetti's little poem:

> What is the beginning? Love. What is the course? Love still.
> What is the goal? The goal is love on the happy hill.
> Is there nothing then but love, search we sky and earth?
> There is nothing out of love hath perpetual worth.

> That day, that Sunday at Mürren, in front of the splendour of the Jungfrau, saw a beginning of love that was to be of 'perpetual worth' and was to have its goal on 'the happy hill', the birth of an unending friendship between John Wilhelm Rowntree and myself. We spent most of that Sunday finding our intellectual and spiritual

contacts, reviewing to one another our past lives and forecasting possible plans for the future. The next morning at two o'clock we started to climb the peak of the Schilthorn together with a little group made up out of the Rowntree party. As John Wilhelm's sight was already dim from a subtle and baffling disease, and as the early morning was still dark, we walked much of the way together side by side, talking eagerly of plans for the future, enjoying the marvellous morning climb and watching the dawning light break over the Jungfrau, Mönch and Eiger to the east of us. We made the summit at eight, had breakfast there, which our guides had carried, and then we took the famous plunge down the mountain on the snow, in the days before the ski had come into use, on burlap sacking. It was a day of continual thrills – my first experience on a high snow mountain – but greater than the joy of climbing or of seeing sunrise on the Jungfrau or of plunging down a mountain top into space was my highborn joy as I went on discovering the remarkable character and quality of the new friend who was walking by my side. We both knew before the day was over that we were to be comrades for the rest of life. . . .

We met at what seems to me, as I look back, about the high-tide period of his young life. He was beginning to sketch out the main lines of his creative work. There were three dominating strands to it. He saw that there must be a new type of Quaker ministry. It must unite *inspiration* and *interpretation*. The creation of that sort of ministry, ministry born out of experience and a knowledge of truth, was his first concern. As a preparation for that type of ministry and service he felt sure that a new kind of educational institution was necessary for training leaders. The creation and development of such an institution was his second concern. And overarching both these aims was his clear insight that there must be a fresh and sound historical interpretation of the entire Quaker movement. He saw that the true historical track had been lost in the mists of controversy and convention, and that someone must rediscover the clue to early Quaker history. This task seemed to be his own particular mission.

I unfolded to him my growing plan to write the history of Christian mysticism and to trace back the roots of Quakerism to those spiritual movements before the birth of George Fox. We both saw in a flash that our two proposed historical lines of study supplemented one another, that our two strands should eventually be woven together and that we were destined to cooperate toward a common and unified end. We talked all these concerns over with enthusiasm and with kindled interest; when we parted at Mürren we had promised to write to each other frequently and we had arranged for future visits to perfect our mutual plans.

Rufus Jones had other holidays in Switzerland 'with companions of the most delightful quality', and these may well have included John; but his next visit to England was in 1901 when he lectured at the Summer School held at Scarborough and lived for four weeks in the Rowntree home at Scalby. 'In our free time,' Rufus recalled, 'especially in the evenings we planned our life work together for a joint interpretation of mysticism and Quakerism, he to specialise in the latter field and I in the former.' John had visited America in 1900, with Rendel Harris and William Charles Braithwaite, to lecture at a Summer School at Haverford. 'I want a tremendous big talk with thee,' he wrote to Rufus, just a month before the Summer School began.

The previous year he had had to write on the death of Rufus's wife:

My dear Friend Rufus Jones,

I was very grieved to see in *The American Friend*, and then in your letter, the news of the death of your dear wife. I cannot pretend to enter into an understanding sympathy with your sorrow, for death has not yet come near me – such a loss is unthinkable to me. But in spirit my heart goes out to you across the water in deepest sympathy of feeling. I feel that, however terrible the blow, you will rise the stronger for it. I know your faith is strong in the Fatherhood of God and such a faith robs death of its sting and changes bitterness and darkness to sweetness and light.

I have you very much on my heart this last few days, and wish I could make this clumsy pen tell you all I really feel. I will not add more – you perhaps divine the rest.

Always with warm love, in which my wife joins,

Your very sincere friend,

J. Wilhelm Rowntree

P.S. I am writing to thee on another sheet on other matters.

The Haverford Summer School no doubt brought the two men closer together, but John did not find letter-writing easy; when he did write the intimacy was obvious, as in his letter of 6th February 1901:

My Dear Man,

It is indeed time that I wrote to you, after all these long months. Often I have had thee in my thoughts, and weekly see the fruit of thy pen in *The American Friend*, but to *write* to thee seems so serious a thing. Merely to get ½ a dozen words on paper at this distance is not enough. And so my good resolutions pick their way along without finding the opportunity where they can make their home.

(The letter continues with much on the Boer War before returning to personal matters – see Chapter 12.)

And now as to thyself. I hear of thee at Harvard – working, of course, too hard, and in consequence overtaken by the blues. When *will* thee learn wisdom? Young America is too impetuous! It needs the curb of sober restraint. I am very glad to see thy address in print – *our* Summer School is now beginning to loom more largely. We begin in August and go on for five weeks, not after the fashion of the last Schools but more along the lines of my Settlement proposal – I am more occupied with preliminaries for it at present. In September we shall come over again, going direct to Chicago – but we *must* see our old friends once more and shall no doubt linger at Philadelphia, etc. for a few days on our way back again. . . .

With very dear love from your friend always – despite his bad correspondence,

John Wilhelm

In August 1901 he wrote again, after the Summer School at which Rufus had lectured:

It was hard work to let you go. It has been an immense stimulus to have you. Your visit has been in the Divine ordering. You have touched people here, and now you will *always* have a warm place in the hearts of English Friends. As for me, I cannot well tell you what your visit has meant and what your friendship means to me,

Always your affectionate John.

On 3rd January 1902 he wrote on his return journey from the States on board *R.M.S. Campania*:

We have had a tempestuous voyage but a speedy. This is a *splendid* sea boat and the seas seem to make no difference to her speed. Only Howard succumbed to mal-de-mer and we have been very comfortable in spite of considerable motion. We arrived at Queenstown at 11.30, and land tomorrow (Saturday) morning at dawn so that we shall not be at the mercy of Sunday trains as you were. We reach the Mersey at midnight and lie in the river till day-break, a comfortable arrangement.

And now a word for thyself from us both. It is not easy to express all one feels either by the pen or by the voice. All during your loneliness we have felt deeply both with you and for you, for we feel that your friendship has grown to be a very close, intimate and precious thing. And now we both feel glad for you in your new-found joy, and believe as the old Friends so happily expressed it that it is in Divine ordering. We look forward to knowing more of the future Mrs Jones, for what little we know is good. May she be a help and comfort to you in the very serious responsibilities which now rest upon you, and which will not lessen with the years. May you both find peace and happiness in the close fellowship of marriage, and may the rich blessing of our Father go always with you and sustain you,

With love your close friends

JW and CMR

Rufus replied at once from Haverford:

It is lovely to think of you in dear old Silverdale with the bairns . . . your friendship is one of the best things I have in my world. . . . You will find Elizabeth a fine soul, wise, solid, level-headed and most loving. . . .

Rufus came over again in 1903 for the opening of Woodbrooke, but learned on arrival of the death of his 11-year-old son Lowell. Once again there was love to support him, as he tells in *The Luminous Trail*:

When the news reached my friend John Wilhelm Rowntree he experienced a profound sense of Divine Presence enfolding him and me, and his comfort and love were an immense help to me in my trial.

Early in 1905 John Wilhelm was to visit his doctor in Chicago again, for his health had deteriorated. Rufus covered his concern in a sprightly invitation:

We are still hoping that the next letter will tell us to 'cool off' one of our rooms for an English visitor from the Yorkshire moors! We will have water in the pitcher duly frozen and the wind shall blow across thy bed all night!

CHAPTER IX

Summer Schools

THE PLANS which John Wilhelm talked over with Rufus Jones at Mürren were already under way. He had written to Lawrence Richardson in October 1894 that he had 'at last finally undertaken the pamphlet campaign', which was to have 'the definite aim of waking up the Society to thought'. William Charles Braithwaite, Edward Grubb and Agnes Smithson joined him in 'a sort of committee', and he was to receive manuscripts, and print and distribute them.

His address at the Manchester Conference was followed by invitations to speak at Quarterly Meetings – Lancs & Cheshire in June 1896, London & Middlesex in January 1897, Bristol & Somerset in February 1897, Warwickshire, Leicester & Staffordshire in March 1897. The success of the Conference had made clear the demand in the Society for lectures on liberal lines, but the development was still too divisive for the official structures of the Society to be used. The Home Mission Committee dropped the subject as soon as the finances of the Conference were cleared up.

The carrying forward of the Manchester movement was left to the enterprise of a handful of Friends, and it may be no accident that they were led by men whose enterprise in business was at this time conspicuously successful – men of energy, intelligence and initiative, who believed that a spiritual renaissance could be as successful as the economic boom they were experiencing in the world of manufacture.

In February 1897 John Wilhelm wrote to George Cadbury:

> If we could get a band of Friends, old and young, together at the same country place for a week, ten days, or a fortnight, arranging for an able course of Lectures of Biblical exegesis, Homiletics, and

on Historical subjects connected with the growth of the spirit of nonconformity, closing the series perhaps by addresses from men like Rendel Harris, John Stephenson Rowntree, Thomas Hodgkin, etc., particularly with reference to our own Society, we may do much to widen the imagination and to stimulate a desire for greater spiritual power and more ability to give it expression. We might do something to stimulate study and to put Friends in touch with the ablest Christian literature of the Age, and to have such a company of Friends met together for a number of days discussing the deepest things of life and all with the one end that they may make their church more vigorous and powerful, can surely have only a helpful influence on the Society. It seems to me, the more I think of it, the School of Theology is worth working for.

He had visited the Cadburys in Birmingham and no doubt talked over these ideas there; later, in Yearly Meeting in 1901 he referred to 'George Cadbury's idea of a Quaker College'. He now talked things over with his father and John Stephenson Rowntree his uncle, and his cousin William Stickney Rowntree, and Fyfe Stewart, who all supported the idea, but he did not think Friends would 'go in numbers to the school of Theology; they are timid and their sense of the need of such an institution is weak'. Friends must start 'in a more private way'. Yet he sought the support of nonconformist leaders like F. A. Russell and Dr Fairbairn, and it was arranged that Edward Worsdell and W. C. Braithwaite were to talk it over with Dr Fairbairn both as to time and lecturers, and then 'secure the men who are thought best for the purpose and also a suitable place of meeting ... print prospectuses and energetically canvass the Friends of enlarged heart and wide outlook to make an effort to come to the School and attend the lectures. He suggested a small committee of W. C. Braithwaite (as secretary), George Cadbury, Wm. Stickney Rowntree 'who is keenly interested and has a wise head' and Edward Worsdell, 'who could work largely by correspondence as they thoroughly understand each other'. He sounded out quite a number of people and was surprised at the warmth with which the proposal was received. George Cadbury replied that it would be right to start with Friends only, and later join with Free Churches to grapple with sacerdotalism, as in the Roman, Anglican and Greek churches it is 'the greatest foe to the spread of real living Christianity'. On 1st March Edward Worsdell wrote to George Cadbury that he had taken W. C. Braithwaite over to Scarborough for 'a long talk and walk with Joshua R.' who was 'clear that stress must be laid on the educational side, and rather as bearing on intelligent First Day teaching than avowedly on the Ministry, lest Friends should be frightened'. A list of 30 to 40 influential Friends was planned as supporters, certain names being omitted 'for good reasons, e.g. J. W. Graham and my own as bogeys', wrote John Wilhelm. He was included, however, as secretary and executive committee member, on Joshua Rowntree's insistence – he found J. W. R. 'now commanding everywhere confidence and respect in a way that four years ago he could not have said that he did'. Scarborough was proposed as the venue, and the School was to last ten days. George Cadbury replied by return: he agreed, but did not like excluding names of those thought 'rather advanced' in their opinions, though he agreed it was wise. He asked for 'a lady's name' to be substituted for his own on the executive committee, e.g. Anne Richardson of Westfield College.

The first Summer School was eventually held at Scarborough between 4th and 18th August (1897) and attended by 400 women and 259 men. Lectures were given both by leading Friends and by leading scholars from outside the Society. Dr R. G. Moulton spoke on the Literary Study of the Bible, Professor Rogers (an Assyriologist from New Jersey) on Buried Cities of the East, Buchanan Gray on Modern Scholarship and the Old Testament, Bernard Grenfell on the Logia of Jesus, Dr R. F. Horton on the Bible and the Spirit, G. A. Smith on Early Hebrew Poetry and on Jonah, and T. R. Glover on Primitive Christianity in the British Isles. Quaker lecturers included Rendel Harris on the New Testament, Thomas Hodgkin on Sacerdotalism, and on the Apostolic Succession, Edward Grubb on Social Problems, John Stephenson Rowntree on the Place of Friends in the Religious Life of England, W. Scarnell Lean on the Revised Version, and Anne Richardson on the Difference between the Socratic and the Christian Standpoint.

Discussion on how the Summer School could be followed up was led by Joseph Rowntree and John W. Graham, and led to the setting up of a Continuation Committee which arranged further Schools (in Birmingham in1899, Scarborough in 1902 and at Woodbrooke in 1903). It also offered courses of lectures in the intervening periods and arranged reading circles, providing a book list of over 90 volumes. The movement spread to America where the first Summer School was held at Haverford in 1900,with John Wilhelm and Rendel Harris both as lecturers. Rufus Jones came over for the second Scarborough school and gave two lecture courses – on the Mystical element in Paul and John, and on Epochs in Christian Thought. This School ran for five weeks and offered a similar variety of subject and a similar line-up of distinguished lecturers as had the first.

Besides a lively interest in the Bible there was demand also for lectures on social questions. The Continuation Committee therefore set up a sub-committee to arrange a Christian Ethics Lecturer List which contained 28 lecturers on a wide range of topics; most were Friends. John Wilhelm offered one or three lectures on John Woolman and the Responsibilities of Wealth.

So began the practice amongst British Friends of gathering in short conferences for religious education, spiritual nurture and fellowship. But rarely have the numbers been so large or the lecturers so distinguished or the hopes so high as in those first Summer Schools.

Rufus Jones in 1901, during his year of study at Harvard

CHAPTER X

West Indies and Mexico

IN THE SPRING of 1898 John Wilhelm undertook a three month visit to the West Indies and Mexico, with Constance as his companion (their two children were five and three, and so could well be left at home) and also Lawrence Richardson. He began his journal of the tour for friends at home* with some reluctance:

> I have not much to say, or to be strictly truthful, not much incli-
> nation for saying it. In this floating temple of indolence good
> resolves melt like butter. You will kindly perceive by the date
> (Sunday February 6. '98, on board *The Atrato*) that I have post-
> poned the strenuous task of writing a diary to the last possible
> moment, in spite of pious vows to the contrary, and even now seek
> every pretext to promote interruptions. I suppose about 12 days
> ago we left Southampton – at least I have a hazy notion of some-
> thing of the sort. Grey skies, cold winds, smooth sea, the Needles,
> a last look at the downs, darkness, dinner, the first heaving of the
> ocean swell and then sleep. That I am told was on Wednesday.
> Thursday and Friday I was reported alive but unconscious.
> Saturday I staggered onto a reeling deck. Mist, moisture, a mild
> breeze, a great heaving leaden moorland all about us.

At times Constance took over the job of diarist: 'John has developed such a capacity for laziness in this climate that he will not write a diary this mail, but says he will just write a postscript to correct all my erro-neous statements.' That was dated Sunday 13.2.98, in Trinidad. John resumed on 27th February on the cargo boat *R.M.S. Dee*, which took them from Grenada to Jamaica:

* The recipients of the journals were – 1. Frank Rowntree (The Cottage, St Mary's), with instructions for it to be read to Acomb Adult School on the Sunday following receipt, 2. John Bowes Morrell, J. Fenwick, Ed. Worsdell at the Cocoa Works, 3. his aunt, Hannah Elizabeth Gillet, 4. Arnold Rowntree, 5. Arthur Sherwell. It was then to be returned to F. Tindle at the Cocoa Works to await J.W.R.'s return. He intended to use the journal as a basis for lectures, but did not keep a copy.

In this climate the diary is peculiarly unpopular – and now it is my turn. So please picture me this Sabbath afternoon in a deck chair, my head on a sumptuous pillow stolen from down below in the reeling depths of the ship. Thermometer somewhere between 80° and 90°, air steaming moist under the powerful influence of the afternoon tropical sun – sea a deep violet blue, flecked with white caps – shoals of flying fish – an occasional big gull, white below and brown above, banks of creamy cumuli in the east and the deck swinging in the most unstable fashion.

The route was partly determined by business interests, as visits to cocoa plantations and references to 'John's experiments' make clear. But apart from occasional notes like 'talked cocoa for two hours' the business side is not reported in the diary, which could be that of ordinary tourists – travelling companions, hosts and hotels, visits to the Pitch Lake in Trinidad, to botanical gardens, and museums, rides in trains, trams and carriages, on horseback and by boat, playing whist 'under the canopy of the stars', Mexican churches, antiquities, food, fiestas, tropical scenery and weather, people and places, all are vividly detailed. For the diary is rich in description, comment and humour, of which only a few examples can be given:

A ride on a tramcar is always interesting. Here a group of coolie labourers, slightly built, with thin arms and legs bare and copper coloured, a white cloth folded about the loins, and possibly short white shirt also and a turban; perhaps some coolie women too, with rings on their toes, in their noses and bracelet after bracelet on their bare arms. Comely women to look at, small and graceful, and with such a carriage. These with their sad pensive and often strikingly refined faces and straight hair are in sharp contrast to the chattering, woolly-pated niggers with their coarse features, obtrusive manners, and overflowing conceit. The nigger is to the white what the Banderlog were to the Jungle people. They reminded you of the Banderlog again and again. They are hopelessly incompetent, incorrigibly idle, overpowering in their conceit and more effervescent than the Parisians. They are however very picturesque and the women who almost invariably dress in snowy white cotton or print dresses carry themselves magnificently and walk like Greek Goddesses.

On a visit to a cocoa estate in the hills of Trinidad, managed for Cadbury's, the representative of Rowntree's was expected to be someone older. The Cadbury manager

expected a venerable and sedate couple and not the youthful couple who actually presented themselves. It appears that a certain cousin

57

of mine who shall be nameless and who visited Ortinola a year before spoke of me with so respectful a reverence that I could desire a larger share of it at home and gave the impression that J. Wilhelm Rowntree was a person of severe and august demeanour.

Sunday 27 at sea, between Venezuela and Jamaica:

Divine service at 10.30 a.m., conducted by the Captain in the saloon, and the responses by the first Officer, the latter mostly in the wrong place. The whole service gabbled through in a quarter of an hour. Still it was an honest bit of seamanship, performed as a duty to Queen and Country, without any pretence or insincerity, all the crew in their best clothes and the Bible on the saloon table reposing on cushions covered by the Union Jack. What could have been more British! We felt the service to be at least as real as the more elaborate performance in York Minster.

March 3 in Jamaica . . .

We were up before daybreak in full riding outfit, breakfasting at 6 o'clock with the dawn peeping in at the windows. Before 6.30 we were mounted on good fresh horses and off to the hills with Mr Capper as our guide. After a sharp canter along the road we were soon picking our way single file along wood paths and zigzagging up mountain slopes. It is quite hopeless to attempt description. The ride was undoubtedly our most wonderful experience from a scenic point of view while in the West Indies. You can add together all I have said of Trinidad and Grenada and you will fall short. In Grenada the mountains rise to about 4,000 ft; here they are over 7,000 ft high and clothed with forests to their summits. We rode up and down, crossing streams, plunging into deep woods ablaze with orchids, past fragrant coffee bushes with their beautiful blossoms, under the clumps of bamboos, and skirted glens choked from cliff to cliff with wonderful feathery tree-ferns whose exquisite fronds trembled in the morning breeze, and ever and again caught wider and yet wider glimpses of the sea. Kingston lay at our feet – a scattering of white on the green plain. Its harbour was like a great still lagoon, sheltered by a long neck of land fringed with the white surf of the ocean swell. . . . Port Royal at its extremity just showed us its red roofs amid the palm trees. At about half past nine we topped the Blue Mountain ridge at an elevation of some 4,000 ft, and lo, there also on the northern side the sea spread out before us. Along the ridge we rode in a keen wind and came all at once upon the white cantonments of the English garrison, the camp of Newcastle. It was very grand among these hills, with the Blue Mountain peak visible not far away and masses of cloud rolling up before 'the Doctor', as the sea breeze which comes here with the morning sun is aptly called. But we could not halt long. Hot with riding up from the plain we only dared in that cooler air to stop long enough to take our lunch, standing by our horses, who seemed to think they had a right to our sandwiches too, and then we were soon riding down a different way home again.

March 4 – Farewell to Jamaica –

and alas, all too soon! Of all islands this is the most delightful and we have all made vows to return there.

There follows a description of the voyage to Mexico, then the 39 hour train ride to Mexico City, the effects of being over 7,000 ft above sea level, Easter in Mexico city, visits to museums, cathedrals, parks and archaeological sites in different parts of the country. Then by train to the United States, reaching New Orleans on 18th April, before proceeding to Chicago. The American colour bar (as in waiting-rooms marked LADIES, GENTLEMEN, AND COLOURED PEOPLE) drew comment:

I suppose coloured people are never ladies and gentlemen. It is strange that I, an Englishman, from a benighted country which still supports such a medieval institution as a monarchy, should find my first sentiment on the Republican and free soil of the States to be one of indignation at the insulting inequality and injustice to a coloured race, who are yet, on paper, free and equal citizens with the whites.

Family Holiday at Aviemore
Back row: —, —, Arnold Rowntree, —. Middle row: —, Connie, John Wilhelm Rowntree, —, —.
Front row: Frank Rowntree, Margaret, Lawrie, —, —

John Wilhelm and Connie with Lawrence b. 1895, Margaret b. 1893,
Antoinette b. 1899 at Silverdale, Scalby, early 1900s

CHAPTER XI

Present Day Papers

THROUGH ALL THESE YEARS John Wilhelm had continued to work at the factory. The firm had become a limited company in 1897, with Joseph Rowntree as chairman and John, Seebohm, Arnold, Frank and John Bowes Morrell the other directors, Theodore A. Rowntree acting as secretary. In this year too the offices at the new Haxby Road works came into use. Work continued at the old factory at Tanner's Moat for several years, which added to organisational difficulties, and the work-force was expanding rapidly – from 1,000 in 1897 to over 2,000 in 1902. But John's health was deteriorating and in 1899 he retired from full-time work, though he remained on the board and on occasion took the chair in his father's absence.

Towards the end of 1899 he moved with his family to live in the village of Scalby, three miles north of Scarborough, first in 'Silverdale', but planning eventually to build. He devoted himself to the garden, beginning to 'intensify cabbages' as he put it. He feared his Quaker work might be restricted, but in fact, at first at least, he was liberated, and wrote in December of 'the spirit which abandons the commercial successes within reach for the advantages of quiet thought and spiritual contemplation'.

The occasional papers of his 'pamphlet campaign' had become a monthly review in January 1899 under his editorship. Six of the earlier essays issued in the previous three years had been reprinted in 1898 under the general title Present Day Papers and formed Volume 1 of the series. The authors were Edward Grubb (2), Catherine Albright, William C. Braithwaite, Joan Mary Fry and Edward Worsdell, who appended a long list of books of modern biblical criticism to his essay on 'The Restoration of the Bible'. Nothing by J.W.R. himself was included.

But once the monthly issues started in 1899 he contributed the main article each month, except in August, as well as a number of book reviews. He had enlisted the help of Henry Bryan Binns, a young Friend living in Acomb, York, both with the practical side of publication and with editorial work. He was five years his junior, and later became known for an intimate study of Walt Whitman and a portrait of Lincoln. He was to contribute verses and an increasing number of articles, especially a series on political and social ideals and an account of the Adult School Movement (the latter in cooperation with J.W.R.).

The January issue began with a Preface declaring a general aim of 'breadth of view and openness to all truth', but avoiding being 'merely destructive or analytical'. The first article, on 'The Outlook', began with an historical review of Quakerism and criticised the evangelical establishment for failing 'the vigorous and cultivated', because it did not 'command the intellect'. Yesterday's truth was 'inefficacious unless it be reborn within the heart of the new generation'. There was a broader evangelism, which recognised conversion as 'a necessary experience in every religious life', though it could be a gradual process; it saw no conflict between religion and science or a love of beauty. The Manchester Conference and the Summer School Movement were 'the latest development of the evangelical spirit', leading to an increase of members for the Society and 'a social religion of brotherhood and cooperative fellowship'. The Quietism of the 18th century had failed because it detached mystical truth from the salvation of the world; evangelicalism failed because it lacked the basis of mysticism. The influence of Rufus can perhaps be seen both in the reference to mysticism and in the desire to hold together the diverging wings of the Society.

Articles throughout the year set forth John Wilhelm's chief concerns, on central religious issues, on peace and social problems, and especially on the religious education of the Society which was needed to maintain an effective ministry. How much Henry Binns contributed is hard to say, but J.W.R. was the editor who dealt with contents, H.B.B. with subscriptions and other matters. The device of the dual editorship was probably more to avoid undue prominence for J.W.R. than to indicate an equal partnership. Perhaps Henry was consulted, helped with research and did some writing, but the impetus was J.W.R.'s and he did most of the writing.

As the Birmingham Summer School approached, however, it became difficult to maintain output. A non-Friend, the Reverend F. A. Russell was invited to write the main article in August (on Robert Barclay), though

John contributed a pungent editorial, attacking the undervaluing of Quakerism, which said we were Christians first and Friends afterwards, and calling for better religious education for the Society out of which an effective lay ministry could spring. This was to be the subject for the main articles for the rest of the year, beginning in September with the paper he read at the Birmingham Summer School on 'The Problem of a Free Ministry'. The October issue was delayed as the necessary research on Friends Schools had not been completed, though it may also have been due to the fact that he was moving house to Scalby. November's issue dealt with Friends Sunday Schools (many Meetings did not have them), and December's with a Plea for a Quaker Settlement. The year's issues (in this and subsequent years) were also published in an attractively bound volume with a line from Whittier on the title page:

And all the windows of my heart I open to the day.

In 1900, however, there was a change of policy. John Wilhelm was now sole Editor, contributing occasional editorial notes and two articles on Our Educational Policy (mainly about Friends Schools); Henry Binns contributed three articles under his own name, but most of the articles and reviews were by others, both Friends (e.g. Catherine Albright, John S. Rowntree, John W. Graham) and non-Friends, including A. S. Peake and W. R. Inge. The magazine clearly had a non-Friend readership, in acknowledgement of which authors' degrees and titles are now given in the contents list.

There are Friends [wrote J.W.R.] in all churches, there are Friends outside the limits of organised Christianity, [who might find common ground in] a re-statement – it may be a new statement – of spiritual religion and of its practical working in society. We seek a positive faith, an interpretation of truth which shall fit close to the facts of life and appeal with the power of the gospel to those upon who the old formulae have lost their hold.

The 1901 series highlighted this aim with the sub-heading on the first page, 'A Monthly Review for the Discussion of Modern Thought and its Application to Christian Thought and Practice'. It drew on the same varied authorship as in the previous year, but also featured a major series by Henry Binns on the History of Social Ideals. J.W.R. contributed a striking essay on 'The Appeal of Religion to the Heart' (Present Day Papers IV 109-13, see pp. 58-9).

In 1902 Henry Binns was once more taken into editorial partnership, especially in a joint history of the Adult School Movement. Output continued as in the previous two years, but this was to be the last volume, as J.W.R. sadly announced in the October issue:

> I deeply regret to announce that it is necessary to suspend the PRESENT DAY PAPERS at the end of this year. I have been for some time under treatment by an American doctor for an eyesight trouble. English doctors had abandoned my case and I anticipated losing my sight. The American treatment is now proving unexpectedly successful. It has, however, entailed severe restrictions, and involves a considerable absence in America during 1903. My doctor has from the commencement looked with disfavour upon my association with the Present Day Papers. He regards quiet and freedom from mental strain as conditions necessary to the success of his regime. I was, however, reluctant to discontinue work to which I felt strongly drawn. But it is now evident that, in justice to the further treatment my doctor has in view and to all circumstances of the case, a suspension of these Papers has become imperative.

He added an expression of his indebtedness to Henry Binns, without whose 'loyal and able assistance' he could not have continued the Papers thus far.

These years saw a maturing of his faith and his contributions to Present Day Papers bear witness to the change. Speaking of hymns towards the end of his life he said that at one time the impersonal hymns like 'O God, our help in ages past' were the most acceptable to him, but that now 'personal hymns came first', and he mentioned 'Jesus lover of my soul' as an instance. He had returned in his ministry to 'the old story of the personal Christ'.

The way was opening, he felt, for a reformed evangelicalism:

> Infuse the new thought with the spirit of the old evangelical and we shall generate a power unfelt since the rise of Methodism. The discovery of the fact of evolution, the rescue of the Bible from the hands of the mere creedmonger and the text-hunter . . . and the closer association of religious ideas with social progress are manifestly shaping the evangelism of the future. Men are feeling their way to a gospel not at war with the facts. (PDP IV 77.)

The movement would be strengthened by the new biblical scholarship:

> A group of scholars have, under the gathering impulse of the scientific spirit, concentrated their energy since the middle of the last century upon problems of biblical interpretation and, by necessary deduction, of Christian theology. Certain broad results have been

attained, involving primarily a changed attitude towards the Bible, which is now regarded with discriminating reverence as a diversified literature of supreme but of varying importance, rather than with blind and unquestioning superstition. At first this movement appeared simply destructive. It seemed as if the foundations of faith were being shaken. But as time went on the positive aspects of criticism became more clearly defined, and those most closely associated with the character of the work accomplished recognised that a new and powerful weapon was being forged for the church. (PDP IV 148.)

Intellectual effort was still needed for Quakerism to fulfil its role:

We are largely ignorant of our heritage and possess but a feeble intellectual grasp on our spiritual ideals. . . . Too much has been made of the undenominational position suggested in the plea for 'Christians first and Friends afterwards' and the statement that it is more important to bring men to Christ than to make them Friends. . . . To make a man a Friend is to give him the spiritual conception of Christ which the world needs. (PDP II August 3-4.)

Quakerism was 'not a refined and exclusive cult suitable only for a race of spiritual exquisites'; it was 'simply a practical and spiritual interpretation of Christ's message to humanity' (PDP V 127). It had a wider message, for there was a 'a remnant of illuminated souls, strenuously labouring for the spiritual an social salvation of mankind'; there was 'a church outside the church . . . men in revolt against religious insincerity, whether intellectual or practical, idealists and doubters, fearless voyagers on the seas of thought, they promise richly for the future. We find them in the heart of miserable places with love in their souls and healing in their hands. They work on though God be a dim distance and the message of Christ an enigma'. (PDP V 29-30.) There were already signs of the political applications that were needed: 'Socialism . . . is a prelude to the profound awakening of the social conscience which we believe to be upon us. . . . the eager, investigating spirit of socialism is the healthier spirit in modern politics, (PDP II April 15).

But the heart of religion was still in personal experience:

The overpowering inrush of new ideas due to the discoveries of science, the development in our Biblical scholarship and even in the theology of the scientific spirit, welcome as these must be to all lovers of truth, have perhaps induced us to part with some precious stones in our eagerness to be rid of the hay and stubble of obsolete ideas. . . . None of our easy verdicts will prove more open to criticism than the sweeping condemnation of the personal element in religion. . . . We cannot transcend our nature. The hands are human which we lift in prayer. Refine away the thought of God till he is lost and unknowable in an all-pervading Essence and you inevitably starve the soul. There is a deep craving of the human heart . . . for a personal knowledge and love of God and for a conscious union with him in thought and action. . . . We may rest for a time upon ethical ideas and seek satisfaction in the Divine Immanence, but there comes a point in experience when these are not enough. . . . The soul stands trembling at the mystery of life. In place of the light which our system of ethics and an impersonal conception of God had seemed to throw at our feet, there is a close and clinging mist. . . . The deepest of our human needs, a living, personal, saving knowledge of God, required to be met through the self expression of the Infinite in terms of character. . . . Christ was the light in the darkness. . . . We must desire and cherish the strong love which is pure gold, which will not be denied, though no ecstatic thrill runs through us, which will not be content with historical or literary or sensuous imagery, but strives in active service and in prayerful contemplation to realise the glory of the living Christ within. (PDP IV 110-113.)

Admire Christ, they say, and you will grow like him; admire him as the ideal of the race, and it matters not whether or no he be the Son of God. The quality of admiration when rightly directed is excellent. But what barren advice for the storm-tossed soul. I do not lack the capacity to admire, I lack the will to imitate and obey. . . . It is true that there are difficulties, real and pressing, in the acceptance of the historical Christ, difficulties of Scripture interpretation, the text, authorship, the possibility of error and myth, the inevitable difficulties of distance and time, but do not forget that there is a living bridge which links us to the past. The present witness of Christ's power in the heart truly yielded to the dominance of his love has a convincing power denied to all the doctrines of the schools. And step by step, generation by generation, we may trace our way through a succession of holy lives to their Divine source, in Jesus of Nazareth. It is the fact not the theory that must convince. Philosophy, criticism, analysis, none can avail against the living testimony of one holy soul. Men have known in their hearts that God is not a silent God. . . . The living personal knowledge of God as revealed in Christ, convicting us of selfishness, searching out our sin, destroying in its pure flame the dross of our lower nature, is an experience which for ever banishes doubt and demands no explanation. It is enough! The heart has felt! It is enough to *feel* that the power of sin is broken and that the will lies plastic to the Master's hand. And to that experience, be it fierce and sudden, or slowly born of lingering pain, there is but one royal road. It is not through Biblical criticism, nor through philosophical speculation, though these have their place. By prayer, the prayer of our whole nature, voicing our abasement and our hope, our weakness and the strength of our striving, our unfitness and our longing, prayer that rises from the very deeps of our being, such prayer alone can pierce the darkness that walls us round, and yield us the joy of the Divine illumination. (PDP V 3-4.)

Henry Isaac Rowntree, 1838-1883

Joshua Rowntree, 1884-1915

CHAPTER XII

The Agony of War

'THE ONLY THING that ever did upset him,' said a member of his Adult School class, 'was to find a scholar in favour of war.' He had, of course, been brought up to support the Quaker peace witness, and one of the earliest talks he gave in visiting other Meetings in 1894 was on the subject of War. But the outbreak of the Boer War in 1899 made pacifism a poignantly pressing issue. His articles in Present Day Papers in May and June of that year were on the Unlawfulness of War and Work for Peace.

> War in the Quaker view [he wrote] is contrary to the spirit of Christ, which takes us beyond the Old Testament and the institutions of Jesus' own time; Christianity applies to the conduct of nations as well as of individuals; self-sacrifice, heroism and discipline, often regarded as military virtues, can be used equally by a disarmed nation; force may be used, as by the police, to suppress evil, as long as it is used in a spirit of justice and brotherhood.

Those who worked for peace needed to prepare themselves by studying the teaching of Jesus, the growth of the rule of law and of humane feeling and of the interdependence of nations. True patriotism condemns actions like the Jameson Raid, takes pride in service, not in armaments, and advocates policies of peace; the church should influence public opinion towards such a spirit, for 'an aroused Christian conscience means an enlightened foreign policy'. The teaching of history in schools must avoid glorifying war and nurture the young in the principles of peace.

When war broke out it oppressed his spirit. As he wrote to friends in January 1990:

> The whole affair is so sickening that it is working upon me like a nightmare. At times I almost wish I were not an Englishman. . . .

The Society of Friends has been lamentably weak upon this wretched war. I have been appalled at the falling away among our younger people especially. I feel that one lesson of the war for us as a church is the need for proper instruction of our *own* people. Each generation has to recapture for itself its spiritual heritage, and we need to seize upon the opportunity this war gives us for the re-statement of our principles in terms which will appeal to a new generation. It is quite a mistake to assume that our young people will grow up 'right upon the war question', unless we take the proper steps to inculcate our principles.

In March he expressed his regret that the official action of our Society as represented by Meeting for Sufferings had been so feeble. (PDP III 15.)

The virulence of feeling against Friends may be judged from the riot which occurred in Scarborough in March, when Cronwright Schreiner, husband of Olive Schreiner, visited the town in the hope of promoting understanding between the British and the Boers. He was welcomed by the Scarborough South African Conciliation Committee in Rowntree & Sons' café, but a mob outside pelted the building with rotten tomatoes and stones. The police persuaded the meeting to disperse, but the crowd pursued them and several Rowntree homes were attacked. Joshua Rowntree, the chairman of the Committee, published a letter of protest, addressed to the people of Scarborough and defending the right to differ-ence of convictions, including the Quaker view that 'the fostering of prejudice and enmity, even to foes, is in the long run hurtful to ourselves, and that injustice to strangers never leads to justice to our own people'.

In December John Wilhelm engaged in a forthright correspondence with church leaders who maintained that war was sanctioned by the New Testament. He quoted the example of slavery which was not specifically forbidden in the Gospels:

For long years ministers of the gospel in the Southern States of America defended the practice of negro slavery with isolated texts. Now all men recognise that, though there is no direct teaching against the holding of slaves in the New Testament, the spirit of the gospel clearly condemns it. To attempt to justify the practice of war by isolated sayings torn from their context or quoted in disre-gard of the clear teaching of the Gospels as a whole is simply to repeat the methods which maintained the practice of slavery in defiance of the spirit of Truth.

He quoted a statement of Canon Newbolt in the *Church Times* that the great war in which we have been engaged had been of the utmost benefit morally and spiritually to England. It had made people serious. John commented: It seems that this carnival of hell in South Africa is to be justified because it had cured us of frivolity. . . . The Christian ideal of life and practice will never be realised if the Church accepts the spirit of the world and refuses to rise above the average of contemporary sentiment and morality.

In an editorial in Present Day Papers in February 1901 on the death of Queen Victoria he spoke appreciatively of the Queen, but added sadly:

> We look back upon the long eventful reign, through the smoke of battle; beneath the universal sympathy for the dead we feel the enmity – of the world. And it is upon a gun carriage that the great Queen is drawn to her grave! How strangely are the pagan strands interwoven with the Christian! How slowly do our people learn!

Then he quoted Shaw's *Caesar and Cleopatra* (published in 1901 after first being produced in Newcastle in 1899) to illustrate the futility of war, concluding with Caesar's words:

> And so to the end of history, murder shall breed murder, always in the name of right and honour and peace, until the gods are tired of blood and create a race that can understand.

The church must alter its attitude towards militarism; in the South African War it had proved wanting. Neither the attitude of the Society of Friends nor of other churches, during the recent trial of faith, will bear much scrutiny. How could they hope for revival, for which they planned?

He had only recently written to Rufus Jones, sharing his distress as is possible only with an intimate friend:

> History's footsteps have been very audible of late. This miserable war has filled our minds with suspense and our hearts with pain, and now with the future dark one can see the poor old Queen sink under the weight of years, made heavier with sorrow. It would be difficult to make you understand, you of the young and hopeful West, bright with the radiance of morning, how sad our people are, and at heart too ashamed and weary of the sanguinary struggle in poor and bleeding South Africa.
>
> We have had a terrible reaction to low and materialistic conceptions of life and duty. May I never live to see such another dark time as this through which we are now painfully emerging. A paralysis has smitten us, and even in our own Society there has been such a moral debacle as I would not have deemed possible two years ago. Our 'khaki election' has shaken my belief in

democracy and opened my eyes to the tremendous and terrifying power of the press. We are in for an epoch in which a new aristocracy of capital will establish a new feudalism of unseen power and exploit the peoples for their own base ends. As for our pulpits, they have been beneath contempt. They have simply registered the passion of the hour, and blessed at the bidding of the politician. We were never in sorer need of the Quaker conception of life, never in sorer case to present our message. You would hardly believe your eyes if you came over here. Thos. Hodgkin's son, a lieutenant though still a nominal Quaker, heads a procession to burn Kruger in effigy. T. Hodgkin makes the speech and Lily Hodgkin lights the faggots. And this at a time when the nation was seething with bitterness against the enemy, and lies and all uncharitableness filled the press. The spirit of war stalked the land, naked, unashamed and our leading Quaker gives his benediction! Don't mistake me. I am not merely complaining that T. Hodgkin takes a different view of the policy which led to the war from that which I do, but I am speaking of the failure to condemn war's passion and hatred, the spirit which breeds strife. The sum of it all is that we have suffered a great moral disaster, and generations will not see the evil worked out again. I wish you were not committed to this wretched Philippine business, or you could have helped us. Now alas! your lips are sealed, and the splendid example which, as the greatest power in the world, you might have given to burdened Europe, is lost. But still there is a silver lining. A remnant in the Society have come through the fire the stronger for testing, and a remnant of the great Liberal party are gathering courage and faith to oppose the false imperialism which, to misquote Milton, is only jingoism writ large. Watch Lloyd George – some say that in 10 years he will be the unquestioned leader of the Liberal forces in the country. People talk of Rosebery – but he is impossible. It will be a disaster if he ever returns to the Liberal party as an official head. He is a mere apostle of force for all his charm. The fact is, Rufus, that our rulers here and in the broad lands of America are under the baneful influence of Otto von Bismark – the Machiavelli of the 19th century, the Napoleon of the moral world as Bonaparte was of the physical. We need to resuscitate the spirit of Joseph Mazzini. Until we can exorcise the Imperialist demon – goodbye to real progress.

At Yearly Meeting in 1901 in the session on the State of the Society, he turned once again to what he saw as the betrayal of Christ by the churches:

If the full meaning of personal allegiance to Christ had been realised, would the late 'just and necessary' war have been possible? There would have been a torrent of denunciation from the Christian pulpit of the policy which led up to it. We had issued a statement of our peace principles, but how little we had done compared with what we might have done, had our hearts been aflame for peace.

He was the first to speak in the session on the peace committee report, expressing his concern at the silence of the church on the subject of war. Was the Society of Friends going to join in that silence? And when the 'Plea for a Peaceable Spirit' was issued by Yearly Meeting it was largely the result of his efforts and drafting.

CHAPTER XIII

The Needs of the Ministry

JOHN WILHELM'S appeal in Yearly Meeting 1893 was not only for personal freedom to doubt, but for ministry in meeting which faced the discoveries of science and of biblical research; knowledge of modern religious thought was needed if the Society was not to fail the cultured and educated – true Quakerism was what was needed by those who were drifting away from orthodox nonconformity, but its message must be in the thought-forms of the age, and deal with what he later called the deeper things of life–

> . . . the mystery of being, the whence and the whither of man, the awful reaches of eternity, the unmeasured solitudes of space, the silent majesty of universal law, irrevocable cause and effect, the iron machinery of fate, the unequal distribution of pain, the sense of sin, the sickening despair of failure, the certainty of death, the apparent silence of God.

(Address to National Adult School Council, 1904.)

The Manchester Conference provided a platform for this new approach, but no official action followed it. He therefore, developed a campaign for an educated Quaker ministry through articles and editorials in Present Day Papers, in talks to Business Meetings, as in January 1897 at London and Middlesex Quarterly Meeting, and in letters and articles in Quaker periodicals. An article in *The Friend* of 11th February 1898 set out his position:

> We are called upon to maintain a principle which is in danger of being undermined, namely the priesthood and responsibilities of the individual worshipper. No people have laid more stress upon

73

this principle than Friends. Its possession has been their strength. Its propagation is their duty.

Such a principle carries with it a direct negative to the insufferable pretensions of the Anglican priest, who poses as the dispenser of the grace of God. It conceives of worship, not as a continuous repetition of prayers and anthems, however beautiful, but as the inward uplifting of the soul seeking communion with God. It contemplates a common priesthood of believers, not restricting the gift of ministry to an imaginary line of Apostolic Successors, but calling upon all men to exercise the gifts they receive direct from the Father of Spirits. It constitutes a universal call to service, emphasising the great truth of the Christian faith that he that loseth his life shall find it, and that through self-sacrifice lies the entrance to the Kingdom. . . .

Our church demands a heavy self-sacrifice. We are, as a rule, busy men and women, with small leisure and moderate incomes. It is no light thing to add the work of a pastor to the life of a citizen. In other churches the congregation leans on the minister. But we dare not set a class apart on the plea of economic division of labour. . . . The work of the church must not be allowed to fall on a few over-burdened shoulders, but must be as widely distributed as our gifts permit. . . . We have dared to take up the responsibility of a free ministry. We believe that in this a principle vital to the health of the Christian church is involved. Then there is no alternative – we must ourselves make the necessary sacrifice. . . .

And what is this necessary sacrifice? Surely it is that surrender of leisure and of other interests which liberates us either for the vocal ministry or the social service of our church. . . . We need to acquaint ourselves with Church history, and particularly with our own, to read the lessons of the past and mark their value for the present. We need to study the Bible in the light of modern scholarship, that we may understand it better and love it and use it more. In these days of restless overstrain we need to secure for ourselves those times of quiet and of mental repose so essential to the deeper and stronger life of the soul. . . . We must no longer ignore the importance of the teaching ministry for which the other churches provide the highest training.

This concern received growing support; in fact the letter sent out in 1899 from Yearly Meeting on Ministry and Oversight might have been written by John Wilhelm himself. After pointing out the general spiritual needs for worship, it declared:

> Many meetings require more of a ministry helpful to those in intellectual doubt, and for this, study and sympathy are alike requisite. . . . We need a wider outlook on men and thought; clearer perception, larger sympathy. And especially we want a fuller consecration of intellectual powers. There is a large field for the teaching ministry. . . . As a Society we must see that our members receive due training in religious knowledge.

He followed this letter up in a paper read at the Birmingham Summer School, which he had published in Present Day Papers in October. He had been to America to study Friends' religious education there and also the pastoral system, but he came back convinced that such development would not be right.

> Paid ministry [he admitted] had the advantages of well-educated clergy, free to devote their energies primarily to the preaching of the gospel. Friends had counterbalancing advantages in the ministry of women, or lay people who could draw on the practical experience of daily work and the spontaneous ministry of those with a prophetic gift like Stephen Grellet and Benjamin Seebohm. But it was necessary 'to command the allegiance of both head and heart'.

He challenged the Quaker dread of what were called 'human arrangements':

> This dread rests upon weighty reasons, but it must be clearly recognised that the characteristic note of the Quaker Meeting, with its cherished freedom of spiritual dependence upon God, is endangered, not only by the intellectual equipment of the ministry, but by its restriction to one man or to one type. (Payment was not the objection, he said elsewhere, but professionalism). . . . It is profoundly true that God does call his servant unexpectedly in the presence of a congregation, and bids him speak unprepared. We may rejoice that Friends have never minimised that supreme prophetic gift. It is also true that no minister can rightly speak without strong conviction when he rises that what he says is said in season, but the deduction that there can be no call during the week and no right preparation of the message is wholly inadmissible. God works in many ways, and Friends living in the freedom of the spirit should be the last to maintain such an artificial limitation.

Many Friends at this time gave prayerful thought during the week to the sermon they might feel led to give in the coming Sunday's meeting for worship. Rufus Jones described, in *The Trail of Life in the Middle Years* (pp 47-9), how he would build up the material for ministry in meeting in his mind during the preceding week – some Friends actually wrote out what they planned to say; John W. Graham described his own similar practice in his *Faith of a Quaker* (1920) pp 245-6. John Wilhelm valued the teaching ministry which such preparation produced and for this reason supported the recording of ministers by monthly meetings. He felt it marked the importance of vocal ministry and encouraged Friends to commit themselves to this form of service. (The practice was discontinued in 1924.)

He looked to Friends Schools to see that the children of Friends were well-grounded in Quakerism, and he wrote two carefully researched articles on the history and present state of the Schools, which appeared in Present Day Papers under the title 'Our Educational Policy'. The Society had begun to grow again, but it drew its recruits mainly from the Adult Schools and Mission Meetings. This made it all the more important for those brought up in the Quaker tradition to be able to contribute from a full and accurate knowledge of that tradition.

But the Schools were in no state to play the part he envisaged. Low as the fees were, poorer Friends could not afford them; teachers were poorly paid and often lacked training. He quotes as an example of the penny pinching methods that were used a book-keeper who had served Ackworth for many years without regular salary; when he retired he was presented with 'an aged horse' which he rode into York and sold for £12. An inspector's report on eight of the Quaker schools (Ackworth, Sidcot, Wigton, Rawdon, Penketh, Ayton, Sibford and Saffron Walden) found a lack of system and finish about much of the work. While English was well taught, there was a mere smattering of many other subjects. Among the assistant masters he found an ignorance of the science of teaching.

There were about 2,000 children of school age in the Society, he estimated, and as many again connected with the Society, so that there were between 4,000 and 5,000 children for whose denominational education Friends were responsible. There were 1,100 places in Friends Schools, but less than 600 were taken by Friends. This suggested 'a doubt whether the Quaker traditions can be effectually maintained where so large a number are not Friends'. Urgent steps therefore needed to be taken, primarily by increased endowment, to ensure that good teachers could be employed and that more Friends could afford to send their children to the Schools, and these he outlined in considerable detail.

A study was also made of Meetings' Sunday School classes and published in Present Day Papers under the title 'the Prophets' Nursery'. Many large Meetings had no classes at all; Quakerism was expected to be picked up in the home. He therefore called for Sunday Schools to be set up in every Meeting, so that the Bible, as understood in Quaker experience, could be taught in properly graded lessons; the history of the spiritual development of the Society should be expounded undogmatically so that underlying principles should be stated as a sort of catechism. There should be preparation classes for teachers under qualified instructors.

For adults the Summer Schools made some provision and the letter from Yearly Meeting Ministers and Elders had commended them; there were also the programmes of lectures arranged by the Continuation Committee. Would it not be possible to appoint Friends who would devote part of their time to study and the rest to visiting meetings to give lectures and courses? (The Home Mission Committee had appointed full-time mission workers, who might perhaps provide a model.) Some of John Wilhelm's sympathisers were able to free themselves for this kind of service, (e.g. Edward Grubb, Neave Brayshaw).

But there was also the need for a permanent Summer School, not a theological college, but a permanent Bible School, which would be for Friends in general, but particularly to develop ministerial gifts. There was a need for Woodbrooke.

Supplement to THE FRIEND, *September 11th, 1903*

WOODBROOKE PERMANENT SETTLEMENT,
SELLY OAK, NEAR BIRMINGHAM.

It is arranged for Woodbrooke to be opened to Settlers on the 13th October, 1903.

Dr. J. Rendel Harris intends by that date to have come into his residence near by, and to take up his position as Director of Studies, whilst Joshua and Isabella A. Rowntree will act as Wardens for the first term, and A. Neave Brayshaw, B.A., will reside in the house.

Whilst preference will be given to Friends coming for longer periods, facilities will be offered, when possible, for shorter visits, ranging from a week upwards. Ample notice should be given.

It is hoped with the minimum of regulations to combine simplicity of organisation, with the best possible help for the differing needs of residents.

Woodbrooke is within easy reach of several meeting for worship, with their many dependent activities, and offers special opportunities for the investigation of Adult School and social work.

It is earnestly desired that an enrichment of the soul, an increase of spiritual power and ability for service, may be the firstfruits of the Settlement.

It is important that the names and addresses of intending Students should be forwarded as soon as may be to the Local Secretary, JOHN H. BARLOW, Selly Oak, near Birmingham, together with some intimation as to any course of study they may desire. This will assist the arrangements which will now be entered upon for Lectures, Classes and Private Study.

The fee will be 25/- per week.

It is proposed, as the accommodation permits, to open Woodbrooke to others who, though not Friends, are yet in general sympathy with the aims and purposes of the Settlement as conducted by Friends.

ORPHANS' PRINTING PRESS, BROAD STREET, LEOMINSTER.

CHAPTER XIV

The Founding of Woodbrooke

FOLLOWING THE SUCCESS of the Summer Schools at Scarborough in 1897 and Birmingham in 1899 there was a demand among Friends for a school for serious religious study. Would there be a place for a permanent one? H. G. Wood, in his account of the origins of Woodbrooke says that:

> The idea occurred to many of the Friends who had taken part in the Manchester Conference. John William Graham, the Principal of Dalton Hall, was among the first to throw out a suggestion of this kind. . . William Charles Braithwaite, who became the first Chairman of the Woodbrooke Council, was deeply interested in the proposal. But the leader who gave most thought to it and who became its most effective advocate was John Wilhelm Rowntree.

Arnold Rowntree, in his *History of Woodbrooke*, says that it was at the time of Yearly Meeting in 1893, that his cousin, J.W.R. had 'visualised a Quaker College at which courses of study might be taken' (though there is no record of him speaking at Y.M. about it), and that after the Manchester Conference 'he at once sought the co-operation of others in a practical attempt to realise it'. Arnold Rowntree was in daily contact with John at the Cocoa Works at this time and they must often have talked about their Quaker concerns.

In the December issue of Present Day Papers in 1899 John wrote his Plea for a Quaker Settlement. He had had exceptional opportunities for studying the pastoral system in America, he said, which had developed because of the failure of the ministry under the old order. Friends, with their spiritual conception of worship and their practical recognition of the common priesthood of all believers could only maintain their distinctive form of ministry if they secured 'a strong spiritual and intellectual grasp upon the fundamental principles of the higher life'. It was a need, he believed, for the Society as a whole:

> We cannot portion off a favoured group and say that these shall have an equipment specially designed for the ministry in which they are to serve; we must make the basis of our education as wide as the church.

What was needed was a permanent Bible School, not a theological college, which would give clearness and force to our spiritual message by placing pointedly before Friends the practical, spiritual and non-sacerdotal aspects of divine truth, in relation to individual and national life. It would be

> a Wayside Inn, a place where the dusty traveller, stepping aside for a moment from the thronged highway shall find refreshment and repose.

The ground for this proposal had been prepared by the article in the September issue on the Problem of the Free Ministry, which closed with a section on the religious training of adult members, which was to be for all members, to provide a rich soil from which ministry may spring. But Summer Schools and occasional lecture courses were not enough. He regarded the five-week Summer School at Scarborough in 1901 as a move towards the more prolonged study that was needed, and urged, as the next step, a two-month summer school which would offer continuous class-work rather than lectures, but what was needed was a permanent Bible School. 'Friends who did not feel themselves called to the ministry would be at liberty to attend, but the curriculum would be aimed mainly at the development of ministerial gifts.' The main areas of study would be the Bible, Church History and Quaker History. The lay character of the School would be kept in mind, and facilities would be offered to those whose means were limited, or who had little time to give. Some would be helped to study at home. Sacrifice of time and effort was needed if the free ministry was to be saved, a point he often made, reflecting his own commitment of time and energy, and sometimes also of health. There was no intention to 'stereotype our worship or to tamper with the freedom of spiritual dependence upon God, but to secure such a general condition of church life that spiritual growth shall be fostered, and a high standard of spiritual intelligence shall be maintained'.

George Cadbury supported the proposal, in a letter to *The British Friend* in May 1901, though in a different form:

> A College for instruction in our own special views as Friends and in Biblical literature, accommodating 100 young men and women

of 17-20 years of age would do more for the Society than boarding schools for the children of wage-earners accommodating 1,000 children.

John W. Graham had regretted the lack of support for the Central School Fund; but George Cadbury did not see boarding schools as an effective way of helping the Society. 'Out of 53 children sent to Sibford by Birmingham P.M. between 1850 and 1879,' he wrote, 'only seven remain Friends'; children educated at home 'for the most part remain loyal to the Society.'

John Wilhelm however still looked to the Society's schools for help, declaring in Yearly Meeting in 1901 that they must have 'a wise and constructive scheme of religious education'. Young people needed our help. 'But it was useless to think that we could do it unless, before they left boarding school, they had some conception of what Quakerism meant. Therefore we must have teachers who were set apart for this work.' But he went on to add: 'If we were really to meet the need we must adopt George Cadbury's idea of a Quaker college.' Elizabeth Cadbury describes how he outlined his dream of a college; then, turning to George Cadbury, he said, 'And I can see the dream made possible and the walls of the college arising, built by George Cadbury.' It would be a noble pile arising on the northern heights of London, with libraries, playing fields and halls of residence; it would be for Friends in business in London to live in, for training teachers in Friends Schools or missionaries at home and abroad – a permanent settlement'. For he believed that there would be a reunion between the Evangelical and Broad schools of thought.

At the summer School at Scarborough in August 1901 he had talks with George Cadbury on possible developments. In November Edward Grubb wrote to George Cadbury suggesting that the Summer School Continuation Committee might be able to help, but he didn't plan to call the committee till J.W.R. got back from the West Indies at the end of the year. John Wilhelm visited Manor House, the home of George and Elizabeth Cadbury in Birmingham, in January 1902. 'He and George have a great talk in the library', wrote Elizabeth in her diary. He met several local Friends, and then the Cadburys offered their former home, Woodbrooke, for use as a college. Henry Lloyd Wilson, who was going to America, was asked to put before Rufus Jones the idea of 'a Quaker Training College'. John Wilhelm took the opportunity to write to his friend (21.1.02) and the next day George Cadbury wrote to him: 'If your letter does not draw Rufus Jones, nothing will.'

When he could not be present at the next meeting on the project, Elizabeth Cadbury commented: 'We look to him as the parent of the scheme and we all miss his wise and loving words.' However, he had drawn up a list of correspondents, and Elizabeth Cadbury notes on 7th and 26th April, and again on 2nd May, 'In the afternoon J. Wilhelm Rowntree and others came to talk again about Woodbrooke; then our local set came to dinner to meet him and further discuss: – decide we must begin quietly'. John Wilhelm then wrote to Rufus Jones, outlining the steps planned for his idea of starting Woodbrooke. He referred to the problem of 'how to train and equip without impairing on the one hand a professional spirit and flavour, and on the other exalting the intellect above the spirit and divorcing the heart in an academic atmosphere from practical sympathy with a work-a-day world. . . . I believe the settlement is a deep religious concern. . . . We are seeking to provide a spiritual revival by *means* of a settlement. . . . We are really asking Friends to take a deeper view of their responsibilities for the ministry, using that term in its widest sense. We have therefore to provoke a spirit of self-sacrifice'. He appealed to Rufus to be the first superintendent for a two year period: 'It may seem much to ask, but I feel that in a very real sense our crisis is yours and that a help-ful solution, which I think is more immediately possible in England than in America, must affect both countries. It certainly means a suspension of your American work . . . but taking long views of the future, I feel that these two years will be far from an ultimate loss to you from the American standpoint, whereas they will be an incalculable gain to us.'

Rufus and Elizabeth Jones came over in August 1902 at the invitation of the Cadburys and visited Scalby ('They will want to spend two or three days with you' wrote George Cadbury, 'I know R.J. greatly enjoyed his stay with you two years ago'). They took part in meetings about Woodbrooke, but Rufus was not able to reply to John's 'Come over to Macedonia and help us' till two months after their return home: it was more important for him to continue his work in America, but he agreed to give the inaugural address and to lecture at the Summer School. It was a bitter disappointment, as John wrote to him on 2nd December: 'It is idle to pretend that your letter is anything less than a severe blow!' Rendel Harris had also been considered for the post. George Cadbury wrote to him on 12th December: 'John W.R. writes me that he has seen thee and opened out the Woodbrooke idea. . . . J.W. has for many years promul-gated a scheme which we hope Woodbrooke will do something to forward.' Rendel Harris came at once to see Woodbrooke and discuss the matter with George Cadbury, and on 7th January John Wilhelm was able to write to George Cadbury of his relief at having secured Rendel Harris, even though he had just been offered a professorship at the University of Leiden.

So plans were already under way. On 3rd January 1903 Elizabeth Cadbury notes, 'Woodbrooke Committee come to tea and discuss Woodbrooke scheme of holding a Summer School there; difficulties of accommodating so many, if as many as went to Scarborough come.' Further committees met on 4th and 20th March, John Wilhelm attending the latter, staying at Manor House and conferring with committee members over breakfast. In April a group of about 50 Friends met; John H. Barlow explained George Cadbury's offer of Woodbrooke with its grounds which he wished to maintain free of cost; £12,000 would be given to provide revenue for a lectureship, and there would be a scheme of scholarships. The Trust deed, drawn up later, explained that Woodbrooke was given

> for the purpose of a College or Hall of Residence or Institution where members of the Society of Friends or Quakers and other persons not being members of the Society of Friends may in the first place receive instruction with regard to and study the Christian religion, especially as it bears upon the doctrines held by the members of the Society of Friends and in connection therewith receive and enjoy the benefit of practical training and experiences in Christian work especially as carried on by the said Society; and secondly study social and economic questions; and thirdly study the classics and theological and psychological and other branches of learning; and fourthly receive the benefit of spiritual and intellectual culture and intercourse, or do any one or more of these things.

John and Mabel Barlow had been living in Woodbrooke while Sunnybrae was being built for them a little up the hill from Woodbrooke. Mabel later wrote:

> I remember so clearly one Sunday afternoon during the autumn [presumably of 1902] cousin George calling upon us. . . 'The Society of Friends needs a more trained ministry, if it is to grow', he said. After discussing the matter for some time, he ended by saying that if, after we left it, Woodbrooke did not let, he thought it would make an excellent place in which to try the experiment.

But by the time the Barlows moved into Sunnybrae, the decision to start the college had been made.

John Wilhelm was sent copies of the report on the 1902 April confer-
ence 'to give or lend to the more thoughtful Friends in each Yearly
Meeting'. Presumably he was visiting his doctor in Chicago and would
call on Friends en route. He was back by 19th July when Rufus and
Elizabeth Jones had arrived in Britain to find a cable saying their son,
Lowell, was ill; news of his death followed immediately, and the Cadburys
wired J.W.R. at once. Rufus went to Scalby on the 21st and travelled to
Woodbrooke the next day for the beginning of the Summer School (23rd
July – 3rd September). He gave his first course of lectures on Present Day
Ideas of God and the Spiritual Life. On the 27th John went home, return-
ing on 4th August with his son Laurie to hear Rufus' last lecture and see
him and Elizabeth off at the station on their return to America.

The Committee meanwhile was preparing for the opening of the first
term at Woodbrooke on 3rd October. Joshua and Isabella Rowntree were
to be the first wardens. An illustrated prospectus was issued giving the
names of a Committee of 28, with John H. Barlow and Edward Grubb
as secretaries. The term began with nine students and ended with 17.
John Wilhelm in lecturing on Medieval Art appealed for research, enquiry
and solid study 'in the intervals of tennis'. He was afraid that the holiday
atmosphere of Summer Schools might spread to the permanent
Settlement. Rendel Harris made the same point in a comment on the
parable of the two sons: 'One son's name was No-Yes, the other's Yes-
No. Yes-No agreed to go to work, but went off to play ping-pong instead.'
Arnold Rowntree later commented that 'at the outset there was some
tendency towards dilettantism'. Another problem was created by the
arrival of three Dutch theological students, who had come to sit at the
feet of Rendel Harris, a purpose rather different from that for which
Woodbrooke had been founded – though it did accord with George
Cadbury's wish for foreign students; for he believed that 'the spirit of
Quakerism would be helpful all the world over, and it would be very
delightful if Woodbrooke could be a meeting-ground for choice souls from
foreign countries'.

He wrote to John Wilhelm, who was in Switzerland, on 14th July
1904: 'I am glad thou feels satisfied with the results at Woodbrooke so
far.' J.W.R., as it happened, wrote to him on the same day much more
fully:

> My Dear Friend George Cadbury,
>
> I have had the privilege of two weeks residence at Woodbrooke
> and have come away, alive indeed, as I always have been, to the

difficulties, but more deeply impressed with the great possibilities of the work. The atmosphere, uniting and deepening in its influence has been remarkable and I have personally felt that the visit has been for me one of rich spiritual blessing. I have had talks, sometimes into the small hours, with many of the young men and have felt that their residence there under the pervading influence of the place has been exactly what they needed. They were as George Fox would say 'tender' and we discussed the fundamentals of faith with perfect freedom, especially gathering in the common room of the chalet after the evening lecture.

I have come away convinced that it is worth a big fight to win a permanent and enduring place for Woodbrooke in the life of our religious society and under a deep sense of gratitude to those whose brains and hearts have given us the opportunities and privileges of this establishment. We do indeed owe you a great debt for all that has been done and for the loving care and wise munificence with which Woodbrooke has been promoted and fostered.

One or two thoughts have presented to my mind during my stay there relative to the future which I should like to put before you.

1. The question of the Dutchmen was apparently acute. It is evident that we shall for some time yet be liable to marked fluctuations in the number of English Friends in residence. The battle for Woodbrooke is only begun and involving as it does a revolution in the Quaker idea of what the responsibility for a Free Ministry means, and a wider outlook upon the world coupled with greater earnestness and faith in service, we must be armed with *patience*. I feel clearer as to the ultimate issues than I have ever done – but it will take time. Meanwhile I feel that it is of real importance that the Dutchmen should never *swamp* the settlement. After all, our concern is primarily with our own and the English Free Churches where our hope and responsibility lie, and I dread exceedingly the intrusion of any *large* foreign element, especially at this stage. I feel that it would be fatal to the whole conception of the place and to the concern which promoted it. This is far from saying that I would *exclude* Dutchmen. On two grounds I think a *limited proportion* advantageous.

(i) They give Rendel Harris students of calibre worthy of his scholarship – not an easy thing to provide in English Quakerism.

(ii) They tend to raise the standard of the work. But I hope that the committee of reference will be able mutually with Rendel

84

Harris to secure a proper proportion and that if at any time (and from time to time this must as yet occasionally happen) it be necessary to secure male students in scholarships that we shall not turn exclusively to Leyden. In this connection I want to make a suggestion.

2. At the present moment we have 120,000 Quakers of one sort and another in America, separated into sections and as a whole drifting apart from English Friends. If it were possible, by scholarships or otherwise, to secure six male American Friends of *any* section, that would, apart from meeting the Dutch difficulty, and providing us with a nucleus for slack times, be a splendid piece of work in itself. It would unite Friends now held apart by old outworn controversies, and it would unite young English and Americans. This latter is an aim I have much at heart as being in itself an end desirable on *both* sides of the Atlantic. Both sides have something to teach each other. I should like to see Woodbrooke a Quaker Mecca, not only for England, but wherever the Quaker name is known. I would write much more but I feel I have already unduly occupied your time. Please forgive a long letter and believe me very sincerely yours

J. Wilhelm Rowntree

Some of the flavour of J.W.R.'s lectures at Woodbrooke on Medieval Art can be gauged from the lectures he gave on 'The Place of Art in Religion and Life'. (See Appendix I.)

CHAPTER XV

The Rise of Quakerism

WITH THE FOUNDING of Woodbrooke John Wilhelm saw one of the two main projects which he had discussed with Rufus Jones, when they first met at Mürren in 1897, well established. There remained the other – 'a fresh and sound historical interpretation of the entire Quaker movement', which Rufus saw as his friend's particular mission. John had for some time been assembling the materials for his research and had amassed a considerable library of Quaker books. He had already shown his belief in thorough research by his articles in Present Day Papers on Adult Schools and on Friends Religious Education. And he was now, in 1904, able to settle at home in Scalby for longer periods of reading and reflection.

He shared the first-fruits of his labour at a Summer School at Kirkbymoorside, arranged for local Friends by Pickering and Hull Monthly Meeting (22nd-28th September 1904), when he gave three lectures on The Rise of Quakerism in Yorkshire. This new development of the Summer School Movement, of holding shorter gatherings for Friends of a smaller area, had begun at Mt Kisco in the state of New York in May 1904. It was intended especially for those who could not get to longer Schools further afield.

He began by acknowledging previous work in the field, on Friends in Thirsk, in York, on the East coast and Hull, and his uncle John S. Rowntree's account of the Quarterly Meeting, and set the scene with a general description of the beginnings of Quakerism. Then follows with much fascinating detail the story of the visits of George Fox to Yorkshire, from the first in 1651 to the twelfth in 1680, and also of William Dewsbury and the first converts, such as Roger Hebden, Thomas Thompson and John Whitehead.

But what was the message that both aroused fierce opposition and won men's hearts? John Wilhelm drew on two pamphlets by John Whitehead for a summary of its essence:

Christ is the light of the world which in conscience makes evil manifest. Those who love sin hate the light, but the light witnesses to their condemnation that it is just. Therefore repent; God's love has power to lead out of darkness. But it must be inwardly felt and experienced. The knowledge of Christ in Jerusalem can do nothing without the knowledge of Christ in the heart. . . . In the strait gate of self-denial you must walk and the daily cross of Christ you must take up or you cannot be a disciple of Christ. . . . God is able to save to the uttermost even while the soul is yet in the body. Let the priests be warned who would put the day of the Lord far off. As for the Scriptures, Whitehead does not undervalue them (in his 'Enmity between the Two Seeds', a pamphlet of 39 pages, there are 277 marginal references to Scripture, both Old and New Testaments), but he seeks rather to show to people the eternal life of which they wrote, which we have seen, felt and handled as they did. . . . So far as they (that is the Scriptures) are free from false transcriptions and corrupt translation (Oh! shade of Rendel Harris!) he owns them to be the very words and true sayings of God. No minister of Christ is made by the will of man, nor fitted for his ministry by humane learning nor sharpness of wit nor by any natural gift, but by the gift of the Spirit of Jesus Christ. Which gift cannot be bought or sold for money, nor limited to times, but is free. As for the ordinances, these are spiritual; baptism is no outward rite but a spiritual experience, the supper is no special meal but communion at a perpetual table of the Lord, feeding on the living bread and drinking into one spirit, which makes us of one heart and of one soul. . . . These are the ordinances of Christ, and these he owns: self denial and the daily cross, love to one another, to do to all men as we would be done to, and not to swear at all, and if any smite thee on one cheek to turn the other, and to feed the hungry and to clothe the naked, and the like.

In his second lecture he turned to the facts and figures, the Meetings established, their numbers, their life as shown in their minute books, their marriages and later their disownments, their discipline, which in the 18th century 'fastened upon Friends the narrowing distinction of external peculiarities, and raised about the fellowship that Chinese wall which, with great labour, we have just beaten down'. Not till the middle of the

19th century was the decrease in numbers checked, and then the wide liberation of spiritual energy at home and abroad, in the Foreign Missions and the Adult Schools, brought with it a quickening of life.

In the third lecture he turned to the lessons to be learned. The movement which in the 17th century was 'exposed to the view and criticism of the world' became a secret society:

> Timidly the Quaker peeps over his hedge of prickly cactus, willing that his plain coat of sleek broadcloth should testify for simplicity, but loath indeed to take it off, like the Methodist, and preach to a storming crowd at the street corner. He is careful to avoid debts and financial disgrace, ponderous in the sobriety of his language and the dullness of his intellect. His culture is narrow, his outlook small; his dinners are good and his worship somnolent.

There had been no serious attempt to set forth the principles of Quakerism between Robert Barclay and Joseph John Gurney, and the Quaker view of truth was still without any adequate modern expression in accessible form. Why could the energy given by Friends to Adult Schools not be enlisted in the expansion of the Quaker fellowship? It was partly a matter of organisation – more local Summer Schools, Quarterly Meetings at which public meetings could be held for spiritual deepening, conferences like the great liberating conference at Manchester:

> . . . appoint and support an organising secretary . . . let him have a useful lending library . . . provide courses of lectures and lecturers . . . call in other Monthly Meetings to combine in the work, and as we take the field, transform our meetings on Ministry and Oversight into missionary conferences.

He ended his lectures with this final appeal:

> Thomas Hancock in his *Peculium* put his finger on a weak spot when he wrote in 1858, 'In 1658 there was not a Quaker living who did not believe Quakerism to be the one only true church of God. In 1858 there is not a Quaker living who does believe it'. We need not make the first claim in rejecting the second. There is a mean between the affirmation and its negative which is possible and legitimate. Thomas Hancock is right – *we don't believe* in Quakerism. That is the trouble. We are Friends for a hundred reasons but the right one. . . .
>
> Please understand me.When I speak of Quakerism, I am speaking, not of the visible body of Friends as they are today. That would scarcely arouse enthusiasm. We compromise too much, accomplish

too little – there are too many dead branches on our little tree. I am speaking of a way of looking at life, of the ideal of what would be if the Quaker view of the gospel, the spiritual, inward view, were realised and understood, not only by the world's people, but by the Children of Light. For it is the Children of Light who do not understand. There is something that has not broken in the heart, some blindness that has not fallen from the eyes. We look too low, we love too little. We are afraid to trust the hidden power of God. . . .

There is room yet for the teaching of the Inward Light, for the witness of a living God, for a reinterpretation of the Christ in lives that shall convict the careless, language that shall convince the doubting. The dust of a busy commerce hides the Cross. The Christ of the people is but a lay figure draped in a many coloured garment of creeds, and, worshipping the counterfeit of its own creation, the world sins on.

There is room yet for a fellowship, all-inclusive in its tender sympathy, drawn close in the loving bondage of sincerity and truth, for noble simplicity of life and manners, rich in true culture and the taste born of knowledge; for a freedom that scorns the flummeries of rank, the perquisites of pride, because it knows the worth of manhood and loves the privilege of friendship; for a simple worship, homely and informal, because intimate and real.

Climb Pendle Hill with Fox and see once again his vision – 'a great people to be gathered'; enter in spirit the dungeons of the past and learn why they were palaces and the bolts precious jewels, repeat again with Nayler his tender words, and in the spirit of his message face the future that lies before you. 'Its crown is meekness, its life is everlasting love unfeigned, it takes its kingdom with entreaty and not with contention and keeps it by lowliness of mind.'

Constance Margaret Rowntree, 1871-1928

CHAPTER XVI

The Valley of Peace

FAILING HEALTH forced retirement from active involvement in the factory. He found the adjustment difficult, as he wrote in September 1899:

It is a discipline, doing nothing, to which I find it hard to yield. . . . Apparently we shall have to leave York soon, and as building is so slow, I am looking to take a country house somewhere, and not to build for a few years. The change in one's life will be considerable, but I quite hope it may have its real compensations. The one thing I dread is to have my work in the Society of Friends restricted. I know it doesn't seem much in any case, but it is what I care most about.

He moved almost immediately to 'Silverdale' in Scalby, three miles north of Scarborough.

He was now able to spend more time at home with Constance and the children. Antoinette (Tony) was born that year; Margaret was six and Laurie four. The closeness of his partnership with Connie is clear from their account of their holiday together in the West Indies and Mexico in the previous year; his affection for the children can be seen, for instance, on the occasion when, although very tired, he insisted on walking home from meeting in Scarborough because he had promised Violet (born at Silverdale in 1903) that he would take her for a walk in her pram. It was a deeply happy home, and though he could speak sharply to the children, ripening years brought a gentler sense of humour.

Yet throughout this period he was often depressed at what he felt was the ineffectiveness of his work. 'Every day at noon till six,' he wrote to a friend in October 1903, 'a depression settles down on me that is hard to shake off.' Unpleasant heart symptoms threatened angina, so that continuing his work demanded considerable effort, as he wrote about the same time: 'I have given the small relics of energy which I could gather to a paper on the ministry.'

Yet Joshua Rowntree, who lived in Scarborough, records that 'his figure which was tall and erect gained in breadth and strength during his country life'. He loved walks over the moors. Sylvanus Thompson for example, describes meeting him in the summer of 1904 for a day-long 14-mile walk:–

> Knowing the country well, he was an excellent guide, only requiring here and there a helping arm where the path was broken and where his sight, excellent in the open air and for the purpose of choosing the road, might betray him into a false step. . . . We struck southwards over the high moor, knee-deep in purple heather. Mile after mile we went, down into Bloody Beck and then towards Falling Foss; then with a long sweep round the hill ridges back to Robin Hood's Bay.

His cousin, Arthur Rowntree, describes the last tramp they had together through the Yorkshire Dales:

> The love of sea and cliff and moor was upon him; the talk was of work for humanity, social and spiritual; his affection for individual men shone through every sentence.

He had written to Rufus Jones in February 1901:

> I am living the life of a recluse at Scalby, reading, writing but not much arithmetic – gardening a little, and walking a little, and longing more than a little to be back at full work. It is hard work saying 'no', and I have been saying it now for so long to everything and everybody. I expand physically, if not mentally or spiritually, and my health remains good. York Meeting has recently (14.11.1900) recorded me a minister, and I do not yet feel at home under this new burden – it will ultimately no doubt come to be a support.

Silverdale remained the editorial office of Present Day Papers until 1902, when medical advice forced the closure of the journal. It was a busy base for the Scarborough Summer School in 1901, Rufus Jones (with his nine-year-old son) staying there for most of the time and talking over their life-work together for a joint interpretation of mysticism and Quakerism.

> It was hard work to let you go [wrote John Wilhelm at the end of August]. It has been an immense stimulus to have you. Your visit has been in the Divine ordering. You have touched people here and now you will *always* have a warm place in the hearts of English

92

Friends. As for me I cannot tell you what your visit has meant and what your friendship means to me.

Always your affectionate   John.

He was already collecting a library for his history of Quakerism – eventually to be of more than 2,000 books and pamphlets: he had begun work on them, marking passages and writing scholarly comments, and during the winter of 1903-4 he laid down the outlines of the work which he expected to take ten years to complete. He had been to America during the summer to see his oculist and had obtained over 200 'essential volumes' with the help of the Haverford College librarian, as he told Norman Penney in July. In November he wrote to Rufus Jones with a draft of the objectives of his 'Study of Quakerism':

(1) To analyse the content of 17th-century Quaker thought, to trace its development through the 18th and 19th centuries, in its relation to the rationalism of the 18th, the modern thought of the 19th and to the evangelical revival of both centuries. Movement such as those provoked by Hannah Barnard, Elias Hicks, J. J. Gurney, J. Wilbur, etc. would be discussed in their connection with the development of central Quaker thought and an endeavour would be made to draw the threads together at the close of the 19th century, so as to present the logical and historical outcome of 17th century Quaker thought in its application to modern problems. (2) To trace the changes and development in church organisation, especially in relation to the practical problem of the free ministry. Such a development as the pastoral system would call for careful analysis and the parallel between Quaker experience and that of the early Christian church would need to be drawn. (3) To trace the relation between Quakerism and the social problem.

The Friends Historical Society was founded in the same year 'for promoting research in a field hitherto but imperfectly worked'. Its journal for May 1904 reported J.W.R.'s plan 'to trace the development of Quaker thought and organisation . . . with a view to the practical bearing upon current Quaker problems.'

He had long felt that Friends' ignorance of their past was a major danger for their future.

A small body like the Society of Friends [he had written in 1899], which has with dramatic suddenness broken down its social barriers and mingled with the world after a century of aloofness must have very clear convictions if it is not to lose its identity.

Young Friends had broken with the evangelical tradition, and many were drifting away, but they would respond to a 'fresh and sound interpretation of the entire Quaker movement'.

> If the fire that lived in George Fox, Edward Burrough and Isaac Penington . . . could only be rekindled; if Quakerism could only arise from the dust and speak to men in the language of the 20th century, there would be such a shaking of dry bones as had not been felt before. It was not to be a revival but a new revelation of the power of the spirit.

He therefore began to work systematically: I shall hope, [he wrote], so to proportion my work day by day as to keep this study going, and at the same time remain sufficiently in touch with contemporary affairs, although undoubtedly this undertaking involves a certain withdrawal from work which would otherwise have been undertaken. I feel clear that if it can be accomplished, having regard to the far distant future, it is the work that needs doing, and may have a direct and practical effect upon the policy of the Society. Naturally, I feel my own limitations acutely, but the sense of the need has rested on my mind for some years, and I feel that it is right to make the attempt.

The establishment of Woodbrooke had necessitated frequent visits by him to Birmingham; visits to see his oculist in Chicago took him from home for longer periods in 1900, 1901 and 1903. He continued to take an active part in Yearly Meetings, and had earlier (in Y.M. 1896) suggested that Y.M. follow the pattern of the Manchester Conference of having special subjects put down for particular times so that Friends could know when they were coming up. Y.M. ought to be more efficient, he maintained, as an organisation of our church life and as a distributor of our spiritual views to the world; the consideration of the State of the Society should be introduced by 'a representative address' or by thoughtful papers on specific subjects. Perhaps there might be concurrent sittings on specific subjects.

He brought his concern to Yorkshire Quarterly Meeting in 1901, and with Edward Worsdell's help he analysed the use of time in Yearly Meeting in 1902 – a sixth of it was spent in reading documents – and suggested measures for shortening Y.M. so that young Friends who were 'doing the aggressive work of the Society' could attend throughout. Y.M. should not always be held in London so that great decisions are made by Friends who either live near Devonshire House or have the money and leisure to spend a good part of a fortnight there.

It was therefore proposed that provincial centres should be used in rotation with London. It would make it possible for many to attend who might otherwise never come in touch with the central life of the Society and afford special opportunities for bringing our views and aims before the public in many of our northern towns. The matter was adjourned to a future Q.M. and eventually Y.M. agreed to hold its 1905 meeting in Leeds, at the invitation of Yorkshire Q.M.

Visits to other Meetings, such as the Free Church Federal Council in Cardiff, on which he reported to *The British Friend*, and lectures and articles both on his central concerns for the free ministry and religious education, and, increasingly, on art, still took time and energy. But by 1904 John and Connie had decided that Scalby was where they wanted to live permanently and plans were made to build a house. He had often remarked that there was a danger in retiring to a comfortable country home of lessening the opportunity to serve others; it was important too that children should not be brought up in seclusion from the world of wider service. In the same way, his father at this time had just devoted much of the profits from the Cocoa business to setting up three Trusts, so that they should not further enrich his family, who were well provided for, but be available for constructive Christian Work. The opportunity came for John when the Executive Committee of the Yorkshire Adult Schools had to give up their experiment of establishing a holiday home for their members. He offered a house with spacious grounds on the edge of the village of Scalby, as a Guest House to be named *Friedensthal* ('the valley of peace') after his grandfather's home in Hamburg (which was probably named after the land in Pyrmont which had belonged to the first Quaker Seebohm). John's own house was to be built on adjoining land (with his cousin Fred Rowntree as architect) and would include a hall large enough for lectures, and on the second floor a dormitory with 15 cubicles to take the overflow from the guest house. A pavilion was planned, for the accommodation of week-end conferences and local summer schools (it was used as a village hall).

Low Hall, as the new family house was named after the old farm which had once been on the site, was an L-shaped building of small red bricks, with square leaded lights to north and east and plain glass to south and west to make the most of magnificent views. The land included peat-cutting rights on the moors which were used to supply the fire in the hall. The cost of the building proved less than the tender and the balance was spent on installing oak panelling in the hall and a fine oak staircase. All that remained of the original farm was a walled garden and a small

Georgian summer-house, to be much enjoyed by the children. Unspoilt countryside stretched away to the west, and to the east also beyond the little village of Scalby, a rich hunting-ground for botanisers in those days. Connie, a good naturalist, enjoyed introducing the children to its treasures; she also developed a large alpine garden at Low Hall.

It was a large house, needing a large staff to run it – some six indoors, as well as three gardeners, a coachman and groom, and the farmer and his two sons who ran the farm. There was also a secretary who, in addition to general office work, looked after the library and serviced the Quaker History project. Management fell to Connie who was a good business woman (being a gifted mathematician must have helped); she did much public work besides, and saw to the education of a number of children besides her own. Both books and music played an important part in family life, each of the children learning an instrument as soon as they were old enough.

Low Hall was a place of peace and of enriching life. In the spacious days before the First World War many of the well-to-do built such homes for themselves; few planned to share their peace with others as John and Connie did. Yet he never lived in it.

Low Hall (as in 1993)
Note mansard windows of domitory where overflow of conference attenders from Friedensthal slept (see end of paragraph two, p.95)

CHAPTER XVII

A Spiritual Testament

ON THE 17th of February 1905 John Wilhelm wrote to Friends in Manchester, Croydon and Darlington to offer a course of six lectures which he had prepared the previous autumn and had given in Scarborough. The lectures, he said, expressed 'in a form less fugitive than an isolated address such a measure of Gospel truth as I have personally been enabled to grasp'. It was the nearest he came to writing a book about his faith.

The first lecture, 'What is worship?', gave recent statistics of church attendance to show that, despite a rising population, the church was failing to maintain its numbers: formal worship was 'smitten with the doom of unreality'.

[Yet] under every form and in every denomination there is true worship, but its truth is inward and intimate in the secret of the soul. The willing abasement of creaturely pride, the concentration of the whole energies of mind and heart upon the highest ends of life, upon purity of thought and motive, upon self-forgetting love, upon Him who in Himself personified for us the holiest instincts of humanity – this is worship – the mingling of prayer and praise, of strife and victory, the hunger and thirst of those who wander in the wilderness, in a desert way, who have found no city of habitation, the praise of men who can thank Jehovah for His loving-kindness, for His wonderful works to the children of men, who have passed in His strength from victory to victory, from the regions of doubt into the sunshine of knowledge, from the loneliness of spiritual isolation to the joy of conscious union with the unseen spirit of the universe. . . . Stand apart at times from outward observance and the spoken word, and in the spirit of inward worship weigh your life, observe its trend, realise its purpose. Give your soul room to grow. Seek the reality which others have won before you and make it your own. The silence of the Quaker meeting means only this. It is no foolish freak of 17th-century fanaticism, but a necessity of the soul's true life. It is not, it ought not to be, the perquisite of any one denomination.

The second lecture dealt with the question 'May we believe in God?' The traditional arguments from causality and design are dismissed as inadequate:–

> The way to God lies not solely or even primarily through intellectual processes of reasoning, but through the heart . . . because we are compelled by the conditions of our nature to think of God in the terms of human relationship. . . . It is God as we see him in Christ who satisfies the longings of the human heart, God the loving father, whose passionate tender care for the least and most insignificant makes the burden of life supportable – brings faith and hope to man. . . . I find it *is* this personal aspect of God which has uplifted and sustained men in the stress of persecution, and given them peace and joy in the bitterness of bereavement or in the article of death. . . . Love is the most intense and active principle in the whole range of spiritual experience. The most loving personality we know is always the strongest in self-sacrifice, the richest in sympathy, the tenderest in charity, the one who enters most deeply into the lives of others. He is never self-centred, he is always reaching out, seeking to serve. This is our human experience. . . . If we say God is love, can His love be less or other than ours. . . . We may believe in God, but it must be an affair of the heart. We must be willing to make the venture of faith, to learn the virtue of self-sacrifice, to take with Christ the form of a servant, and with him to live within self-imposed limits for the sake of doing good. Step by step as we approach Christ experimentally, see with his eyes of tender pity, feel with his heart the burden of the world, we shall be learning to know the Father.

The third lecture, 'Is the Bible Inspired?' was never delivered, owing to the death of his brother-in-law Henry Ernest Grace, and another Friend spoke for him in the Scarborough series. The argument was, however, summarised in the final lecture:

> The Bible is the gathered literature of a people, intensely human, wide in its range and variety, unequal in its spiritual value. Its

inspiration is to be judged by the simple test of its ability to inspire, and its value lies, not in its supposed infallibility, but in its record of phenomena unique in human experience, illustrating the working of God in the human heart, and, above all, the message, life and death of Jesus Christ, and the beginnings of the Christian Church. The theory of an infallible text is purely mechanical, not spiritual, and inasmuch as the theory dehumanises the Bible, while distorting its really Divine quality into a parody of the fact, it has worked untold mischief, destroying the sense of reality and lowering the Bible to the level of an idol or a fetish. We may indeed welcome in the higher critic and all that he signifies a return to an intelligent belief in the divine worth of the Scriptures, confident that scholarly and reverent study of material so rich in spiritual teaching must be increasingly fruitful. Truth can never be destroyed; in the fairest light of criticism it can never suffer. . . .

If some misconceptions have to be removed, if here we took for history what was really folk-lore, or there we read as canonical a text that was interpolated, faith will ultimately be clearer and stronger for the correction. But of this we may be perfectly sure that whatever may be the ultimate results of the development of honest, scientific Biblical criticism, nothing can eliminate the person of Jesus nor weaken the value of a single text which is spiritually true. . . . The evidence for Jesus does not rest upon the Gospels alone, it rests also upon the history of 2,000 years, a history unintelligible and impossible apart from him, and finally upon the living witness of the heart, a combined testimony which must increasingly vindicate the broad, substantial truth of the Gospel records.

(In an article written about the same time for *The Friends Quarterly Examiner* he related this topic to the thought of early Friends:

The thought-stuff of Fox, Penington and Barclay was never properly worked out. We never understood the Inward Light. This throws us back on the Inward Voice as the ultimate arbiter even of the Bible. Is this to mean, as Lecky drily suggests, 'the deification of a strong internal persuasion?' The difficulties of the doctrine of Inward Guidance are . . . serious and practical. I would suggest that the solution lies in a deeper interpretation of the person and message of Jesus Christ.)

In the fourth lecture he faced the question, 'What has Jesus to say to the individual?'

We talk of Jesus as the Son [he said]. Certainly he was the Son in his relation of perfect filial obedience to the Father, a relation in which he is for us the Way, the Truth and the Life, but I think we miss the deep significance of the Cross, if we set Jesus in antithesis to God and press the symbolism of son too far. 'I and the Father are one.' That means to me that I think of God in terms of Jesus Christ, that I pray to Jesus as representing the Father to my consciousness, or to the Father as I see him in Jesus. Carry that thought to Calvary itself. See in the crucifixion not merely a martyr's death, not merely a passing gleam of God's love, certainly not a sacrifice to God carrying a legal significance, but in truth the flashing light of an eternal fact, the nature of God's relation to sin, of the pain we inflict on his heart by our own wrong doing. Here is the wonderful dynamic of the Cross. God calls you to him. He shows you his suffering, he shows you the hatefulness of the sin that caused it, and in showing you his love, shows you the punishment of alienation from him, the hell of the unrepentant, in which he must remain until repentance opens the gate for the prodigal and gives entrance to the free forgiveness and love of the Father's house. In Jesus, in his life and in his death upon the Cross, we are shown the nature of God and the possibilities that are within our reach. We are shown the world as the Father sees it, are called to live in harmony with his will and purpose, to hate the sins that made him mourn, to scale the barrier of sin and discover that the way of penitence lies open and direct to the Fatherly heart. No legal bargain, but a spiritual conflict, an inward change, the rejection of the living death of sin, the choice of the new birth, of the purified self, the conversion from a low and earthly to a high and spiritual standard of life and conduct – here you have the practical conditions of salvation, and in the active, free and holy love of God, ever seeking entrance, ever powerful if we but yield the gateway of our heart, is the substance of the gospel. The revelation of God's Fatherhood and the possibility of unity with him through Christ meet the deep need of the soul for a centre of repose apart from the transitory interests and the things of time.

In his fifth lecture he asked 'What has Jesus to say to the State?' He based his answer on the nature of Christian Love:

God is social, man is social, because God is love, and because love expresses itself through personal relationships. . . If the Fatherhood of God is real, and the brotherhood of man means that all men are the children of God, then the term brotherhood covers the whole human race. . . . There is no national limit to the family of God. . . . It is the duty of the Christian Church to realise in common experience and intercourse the ideal of her Master. Were she consistent to his teaching, the armies of Europe would melt like snow in spring-time, and the vast enginery of war pass like an evil dream. . . .

After quoting from his brother Seebohm's study of poverty in York that 'the wages paid for unskilled labour are insufficient to provide food, shelter and clothing adequate to maintain a family of moderate size in a state of bare physical efficiency', he goes on:

We cannot live to ourselves, even if we would. It matters infinitely *how* we live to others. Rooted in the love and power of Christ we shall not dare to be satisfied with spasmodic service. Brotherhood is not a question of bazaars, or subscriptions, of occasional charities paid as doles to conscience, or the gifts of lightly missed etceteras from the full basket of pleasure. It is the question of a life of stewardship given in all its energies and purposes to the common good.

In the final lecture he summarised the argument of the course as a whole, and finished by turning to personal experience, 'for we are here at the intensely personal centre of all religion'.

The conventionally religious person may be deeply touched sometimes, as at the death of a friend. But let us suppose that the strong blow of some great catastrophe were to strike me. Something that destroyed the routine of self-pleasing and compelled me to face the realities which I have so steadfastly shirked. Let it be some permanent restriction like blindness, or some financial disaster involving penury – no matter what. . . . How are we to be saved? . . . Beyond all question a first consideration is sincerity . . . we must honestly seek the true life, we must honestly wish to escape the toils of self love. . . . I turn to Christ, the Christ of the Gospels. What is salvation by Christ? It is nothing mysterious, it is to be made like unto him. 'From morning to night keep Jesus in thy Heart, long for Nothing, desire Nothing, hope for Nothing but to have all that is within thee changed into the Spirit and Temper of the Holy Jesus' (William Law). . . . Here we have the method, not only of the mystic, but of every soul who has sought God through Christ. . . . But we must know the *steps* of this pilgrim's progress. Let me state the case again in terms of personal experience. I determine to seek this peace of God till I find it. My sincerity is not to be doubted. I am earnest

101

in my quest. So far so good. . . . I want to get away from the prison of my selfishness. I want to realise love. But I am not going to do it by mere mortifications and penances. In my desire to practice self-sacrifice I am in danger of confounding the mutilated life of the ascetic with the cross and discipline of Christ. I am right in thinking that the worldly life full of self-indulgence is a small and contemptible life; I am wrong in thinking that the Christian life consists merely in not doing things that other people do. The Christian life is not an empty garret but a place beautiful by the side of which the life of the most sumptuous sybarite is a wretched hovel. Moreover mortification of this sort breeds a judging temper and a spirit of pride. Self-sacrifice is self-realisation. I must approach my holy experiment from another side. I must seek not merely to lop off but to grow. I must acquire something I have not got. And here is a difficulty. In practical experience how am I to know what is meant by listening to the voice of Christ, obeying him and following him? How am I to identify the substance behind the current phrasing of the religious in my own inner consciousness? At first indeed there may be nothing to recognise, no intimation of divine power, no distinct voice thrilling and commanding the soul, no presence before whom I instinctively kneel. No, perhaps not. But there is conscience, and conscience is a guide I can follow. For example: be thoughtful of others, even in little things; make a practice of forgetting yourself. In the past it was always *I*, what do they say and think of *me*, am I getting the recognition that is my due? Now let it be otherwise. Am I helping him, what can I do for him, what am I thinking of him? Am I giving him his due? Without cessation, in the intimacies of home life or on the broad stage of public service, the choice between recognised alternatives recurs. Generally I know perfectly well which is the right choice. Someone angers me, insults me. I want to hit back, sting with a sharp repartee, crush with a jibe. I practice restraint, I return soft answers. . . .

But I cannot rest satisfied here. I seek not only discipline but victory. I want to know not only conscience, but Christ. Yes, but to the sincere experimentalist, using his conscience as a guide and seeking always to focus his life on that of Jesus Christ as he knows him in the Gospels and recognises him in his faithful disciples, there comes a time when the line between conscience and Christ grows very thin. There comes a time when the higher life of which I am always aware, and which I have tried to follow, becomes so merged in my thought of Christ and my devotion to him, that I can hardly distinguish the two in my mind. There comes a time when suddenly I am on my knees, my whole soul flooded with light and love, tears in my heart and eyes, an unspeakable peace enfolding me. The pierced hands have reached through to me at last and drawn me gently forth to him. . . .

I have sketched, you say, a hypothetical career. No, it is a story from real life. You say I have spoken in mystical language. I answer, Yes, the supreme moment cannot be defined in the dry language of theology, nor can words express it. You say the experience is the result of mental suggestion practised over a term of years. I answer, no-one believes that who has once been there and taken off his shoes on holy ground – the reality is too overpowering, the effect too profound. But is this the experience of everyone who tries the experiment? That question needs a careful answer. There are for example degrees in the sincerity and earnestness with which the experiment is pursued, and we must consider the great variety of temperament, no two individuals seeing life with the same eyes. I think the true answer is this, that the measure of God's response is the urgency and strength of our appeal, but it would be mischievous to assert that the character of the response always bears the same identity. I believe experience shows on the contrary that the character of the response is conditioned by individual needs, though in its substance it must always be the same – the consciousness, more or less clear, of union with God in thought and action, of an eternal purpose and worth in human life, and of all embracing love. This union and sense of love, if experience be a guide, is strongest and deepest where the thought of God has been focused in the personality of Jesus Christ.

But perhaps I have made haste too fast. If I go back to my pilgrim, I find in his experience something upon which I have not touched. It is not a smooth progress that he makes. His sincerity wavers before the fierce resistance of hereditary evil, ingrained selfishness, natural sloth. There are times when he cannot keep his eyes upon the cross, when the goal upon which he set his heart grows dim, when the baser self yearns for the flesh pots of Egypt. How can he win through? There is only one way, the way of prayer. I do not mean formal praying, the rapid gabbling of the Lord's Prayer, or the set petition for outward benefits. I mean the prayer of sinful man crying from the depths of his great need, 'Create in me a clean heart, O God, and renew a right spirit within me'; the prayer of the longing soul seeking to escape from the clog of fleshly imperfection and to breathe the free pure air of the spiritual life. Such prayer to be potent must be personal, it must throb with the conviction of human helplessness and of God's power to save, it must spring from a heart in which deep emotion has broken the reserve of pride. And while in its supreme expression such prayer may be only occasional, victory will be finally won only by the continuous cultivation of the prayerful spirit. In the spiritual athlete prayer becomes a habit of mind, not a spasmodic exercise. It becomes indeed the sign-manual of the soul's intimacy with God. (For the full text see *Essays and Addresses*, 299-405.)

Friedensthal as at March 1993

CHAPTER XVIII

Facing Death

THE LAST ARTICLES by John Wilhelm Rowntree to be published were appreciations of friends whose lives had been prematurely cut short. His brother-in-law Henry Ernest Grace died suddenly at the age of 34, and he was asked to write the obituary which appeared as the leading article in *The Friend* on 2nd December 1904. It was a bitter blow to the family, as he began by saying:

> Death may seem ruthless and unmeaning when, as with the savage stroke of a knife, a service rich in achievement and promise is cut untimely short: but the love of God shone so unmistakably through the life thus taken that, even in the sharp pain of bereavement, we can say with trustful resignation – Thy will be done.

Then followed an account of a life which mirrored his own remarkably, for Ernest Grace, born in May 1870, had gone to school at Bootham (1885-87), married Winifred Naish, Constance's elder sister, in August 1895, worked long and successfully for the Adult Schools in Bristol, and combined a deep seriousness with a vigorous love of fun:

> To the last he was ardent and boyish. Pressed with the serious duties of an extensive business, and under a profound sense of the realities of the common human need, he could enjoy a game of cricket like a schoolboy, and would go miles to see a fire. Serious under his gaiety, he was never afraid of fun, and had a quick and saving sense of humour, a genial laugh for the little oddities and foibles of human nature. But his roots went deep.

John's last article appeared in the magazine of Bootham School in February 1905. It was prompted by the early deaths of several Old Scholars:

Their life-work just begun [he wrote] has been abruptly cut short and we still feel the pang of parting, feel perhaps as an intolerable burden the weight of that dark mystery of life which grows no less with the gathering years. . . . One is tempted at times to take hard views of God and fall back upon a self-contained stoicism as the only way of life. . . . We may reverence Marcus Aurelius, that granite peak in a range of ignoble hills, but to insist that his brave spirit can teach us an all-sufficient philosophy is to deny the most obvious facts of experience. Nay! the very lives taken from us call us to a sunnier view of faith, a stronger belief in the dignity and purpose of being. Courage, unselfishness and above all love, that root of faith and unity of all the virtues, found in them their witness. Every man knows in his heart that there is no greater thing in the world than unselfish love. Death cannot conquer, nay, he teaches ever that love is supreme. Good men do not die. Their lives are as the tearing of the veil, they show us something of that which is eternal, for if here love is greatest in the heart of man, must it not be greatest in God Himself? And if greatest in Himself, then let the mystery of his will be never so dark, we may gird ourselves each to his life's work with something more than courage. Love bridges death. We are comrades of those who are gone; though death separate us, their work, their fortitude, their love shall be ours and we will adventure with hope and in the spirit and strength of our great Comrade of Galilee, who was acquainted with grief and knew the shadows of Gethsemane, to fight the good fight of faith.

Early in 1905 his sight was again causing anxiety – his central vision was 'better than ever', but he had lost two thirds of the outer vision gained when last in Chicago so he agreed to another visit to his American specialist. For himself he would have preferred to stay at home and take the risk, but felt that for his work he must seek the best help available. Before leaving he fulfilled all the outstanding engagements that he could: one was a lantern lecture on 'The Atlantic Ferry' to the Malton Adult School – 'the whole lecture was brimful of fun, and the audience, many of whom heard him for the first time, were quite carried away by the charm of it'. His last Sunday in England was spent in York, where he spoke to his old class at the Acomb Adult School, and gave the address at the laying of the foundation stone of a new Adult School in Burton Stone Lane. A grand sunrise had suggested a passage in I Thess. 5 and he dwelt on the light as revealing love to man in the love of God. This was followed by ministry in the Meeting House on the victory of faith, leading from simple beginnings to 'life on the heights', whilst in touch with humanity in the valley. He closed by quoting the hymn

Heaven's morning breaks and earth's vain shadows flee;
In life, in death, O Lord, abide with me.

When he was about to sail, he had a bout of flu, but treatment seemed successful and he and Constance embarked on *The Caronia* on 25th February as they planned. The boat stopped at Cobh and he stayed up on deck to see the mailbags loaded and then to watch the receding Irish coast. In doing so, he caught cold, of which he made little at first, and enlivened his table in the saloon with typical wit and a fund of 'tall' Atlantic Ferry stories. But before long pneumonia developed; complications followed and he became delirious. When Rufus Jones met the boat at New York, John did not recognise him; he was rushed to hospital, but only lived three or four days longer. He was buried in the Friends Burial Ground at Haverford, where Rufus Jones lived. The funeral brought together many Friends of both branches of the Society, whose divisions he had so longed in his life to see healed.

Arnold Rowntree took the next available boat to cross the Atlantic, visit his cousin's grave with Constance and bring her home. They were met at Plymouth by her brother Duncan, and travelled back to York together.

The sense of loss is the same to us all [Arnold wrote later]. It is terribly hard to think of facing all the problems in future without the man who has led and inspired us, and who was so close to one that we told him all – our worst as well as our best – and always got help. Who will interpret to us the divine revelation as he has done?

At one of John Wilhelm's lectures at Kirkbymoorside in the previous autumn he had spoken of the bitterness of bereavement:

I know absolutely nothing of a previous existence, absolutely nothing at first hand of a future existence. . . . I see no home lights in the gloaming shining for me, and yet however I may long to dismount from my machine of life, however much I may dread my goal, I *must* go on. Must, and the darkness is very great. For example, I love someone dearly, my whole life is wrapped up in that life, the life of my friend, in closest unity of heart and sentiment. Suddenly in a few days, in a few hours, an unforeseen disease develops. Death strikes with a savage knife. That friend is taken from me. I hear nothing, I see nothing more of him. I do not know where he is gone. I am left alone. All the little things we did and planned together bring a sharp pain to the heart as I think of them. They can never be again. Never. The future is desolate, the present is filled with an intolerable ache of hopeless longing.

So must Constance and his friends have felt. Could they remember the comfort he had found? Others had suffered in the same way and had passed through a similar experience into a holy place:

How can they be peaceful and patient when you are hopeless and sad? Question them. They will tell you that the love of Jesus Christ has comforted them, that in learning to know him they have learnt to know God as a loving Father, that the presence of his love and the sense of his sympathy is so real and abiding that against the seeming cruelty of a bitter bereavement there is no rebellion but through it all a sense of sweet surrender to a heavenly will.

Rufus Jones spoke for many of the young Friends who felt that they had lost their foremost leader when he tried to express what John Wilhelm's life and friendship had meant to him:

His intense convictions, his glowing faith, his sense of reality, his passion for the supreme ideals of Quakerism, his experience of God, the depth of his worship, the sweep of his prayers, the power of his personality – all these things captured me and gave me fresh inspiration for life and for service.

His going [he wrote a few days after his death] has cast a shadow on many of our lives, it has made all our tasks harder and it has left us much poorer, but his banner shall not fall, and what he lived to do shall with Christ's help be carried on by the band of faithful friends who have felt the inspiration of his life and who have had visions of the goal towards which he was pressing.

108

CHAPTER XIX

The Work Goes On

NO ONE CAN TELL what the death of John Wilhelm meant to those who loved him. The Society of Friends mourned a prophet of vision and concern, but his family and friends had lost a lively and loving personality, whose company was fun, whose wisdom was always ready to be shared, whose faith had faced doubt honestly and risen triumphantly over suffering.

Yearly Meeting was held in Leeds in the shadow of his loss, and quoted his words in the Epistle. However it was stimulated by the occasion of meeting outside London for the first time in 230 years, with its pattern changing into its 20th-century form.

> It was an awe-inspiring experience [wrote Elfrida Vipont Foulds]. Drawn together by a common tragedy and shaken from their accustomed ways by new meeting places and new surroundings, Friends threw aside their customary caution and restraint and rejoiced in a new sense of fellowship.

Friedensthal was opened in 1905 as planned, and the gatherings arranged for Low Hall were carried through by Connie, with the help especially of John's cousin Arnold, and a week-end meeting of Adult School leaders from all over the country soon after Yearly Meeting made a successful start. There were over 300 residents in the first season. The venture was a great success, and by 1919 it was clear that larger premises were needed. Court Green in nearby Cloughton, and then the adjacent Cober Hill, were bought; together they could take 100 residents. Cober Hill has now served Friends and others for over 70 years; the annual Easter Settlement held there by Yorkshire General Meeting can trace its origin directly to the initiative of J.W.R.

Joshua Rowntree, living in Scarborough, was able to help Connie in many ways. He also edited a selection of John Wilhelm's writings and published them with a memoir of his life before the year was out. *Essays & Addresses*, as the book was called, was to be the chief printed vehicle of his thinking for many years. Its success encouraged Joshua to produce a second volume *Palestine Notes*, which gave extracts of his travel journals, lectures on art and notes for adult school lessons, as well as further addresses: it showed something of the human side of J.W.R. which *Essays & Addresses* missed.

In September a meeting was held at Scalby to consider the continuation of his plans for a history of Quakerism, on which Joseph Rowntree had consulted Connie. Four members of the Rowntree family, Joseph, John Stephenson, Seebohm and Arnold, met with Rufus Jones, Edmund Harvey, Neave Brayshaw and William Charles Braithwaite. It was agreed that the work was to be shared between Rufus Jones and W. C. Braithwaite and generous financial help was promised from the newly formed Joseph Rowntree Charitable Trust. The result, which became known as the Rowntree Series of Quaker Histories, came to be recognised as the standard work and had an incalculable influence on British Quakerism. William Charles Braithwaite's *Beginnings of Quakerism* appeared in 1912 and his *Second Period of Quakerism* seven years later; Rufus Jones' *Later Periods* was published in 1921 – he had already contributed *Quakerism in the American Colonies*, and *Studies in Mystical Religion* and *Spiritual Reformers in the 16th & 17th Centuries* amply fulfilled his part in the original plan by which J.W.R. was to deal with the history and he with the mystical antecedents.

Other Quaker histories were written in the years following, notably A. Neave Brayshaw's *The Quakers: Their Story and Message* (1921): all owe a considerable debt to the Rowntree Series.

Quaker bookshelves were also to be enriched by other writings of J.W.R.'s friends: Edmund Harvey's *Rise of the Quakers* appeared in 1905, Edward Grubb's *Authority and the Light Within* in 1908, J.W. Graham's *Faith of a Quaker* in 1920. Rendel Harris, Edward Grubb and Rufus Jones all wrote much that Friends valued and that took Quaker thinking to a wider public.

Another conference held at Scalby later the same September carried forward the concern for Quaker Tramps, which had been mooted informally amongst a few of J.W.R.'s closest friends. Arnold and Arthur Rowntree made the preliminary arrangements and Wilfrid Crosland planned accommodation and routes in six areas – Wensleydale,

Nidderdale, Airedale, Pendle Forest, Pickering and Whitby, and Osmotherly. A preliminary conference was held at Scalby and a closing meeting in York. Public meetings were held en route and many personal contacts made. A permanent result of the movement was the Yorkshire 1905 Committee set up under Arnold Rowntree's chairmanship to carry on the work of extension which J.W.R. had been planning shortly before his death: the name commemorated both that event and the holding of Yearly Meeting in the county.

J.W.R. was one of the first Trustees of the Charitable Trust set up by his father in 1904. He did not attend the first meeting of Trustees in December 1904, and the second recorded his death. Yet his work was carried on by much that they did; their minutes make clear that they often had his concerns in mind. His friend Edward Grubb was employed at the second meeting to give 'religious teaching to members of the Society of Friends and those associated with them in worship or Christian work . . . on lines which would have commended themselves to J.W.R.' When finance was arranged for the Quaker History project, it was as 'a work to which John Wilhelm attached such great importance and which he had so much at heart'.

Financial help was regularly given to Woodbrooke in grants to enable individuals to study there, in providing the salary for a lecturer in economics and for H. W. Waller to work as librarian (money was also given for books). Help was given in meeting an early deficit in working expenses, but the policy outlined in the Trust deed excluded contributions towards new buildings.

£250 per annum for three years was offered to the Woodbrooke Extension Committee when it was set up (1907) and also to the proposed annual Swarthmore Lecture which W. Charles Braithwaite and Arnold Rowntree advocated and which the Extension Committee was asked to arrange. Rufus Jones was invited to give the first lecture (in 1908, on Quakerism, a Religion of Life), and subsequent lecturers were Friends to whom J.W.R. had been close – W. C. Braithwaite, Joan Mary Fry, Thomas Hodgkin, Edward Grubb.

The Trustees saw a clear distinction between the mission meetings run by Home Mission workers under the Home Mission Committee and the projects for religious education which J.W.R. had set in train. They therefore encouraged continuation of Summer Schools, which Edward Grubb was active in arranging (e.g. in Guildford, Kendal, Glasgow) and also in week-end lecture schools and series of addresses. In Yorkshire the 1905 Committee undertook similar extension work: Foster Brady of

111

Barnsley, after a period at Woodbrooke, became Assistant Secretary and worked mainly in the Pontefract Monthly Meeting area.

A joint Committee of Leeds M.M. and the 1905 Committee established a non-residential Settlement in Leeds in 1909 to provide locally the kind of religious education offered by Woodbrooke. Arnold Rowntree reported to the Trustees on the need for such a settlement, where Friends and others coming within their sphere of influence, particularly the children of Friends, could attend lectures on religious, social and economic questions and be given some of the advantages of institutional life without actually entering into residence at a settlement. Leeds Friends had not the financial resources to run the project (only four families in Leeds Meeting now kept two or more servants), so grants were agreed for salaries, and Arnold Rowntree arranged to pay the rent of a suitable house. Gerald Hibbert was appointed Warden and Maurice Rowntree (Joshua's son) sub-warden; both took part in extension work outside Leeds as well as lecturing at the Settlement. About the same time a similar Settlement was started at 21 St Mary's, York. Other Settlements were founded in other centres, and in 1920 a gathering of interested Friends at Cober Hill founded the Educational Settlements Association, with Arnold Rowntree as its chairman. The Association was recognised by the Board of Education in 1924, and the Settlement idea was accepted in the 1944 Education Act as part of the national education system, but by then the Settlements had moved on from their original religious purpose to a broadly cultural role.

Meanwhile Connie had picked up the threads of life at Low Hall. She was deeply religious, sharing John's strong faith, and did not allow herself to be crippled by a sense of loss. She found great happiness in her family, increased by the birth of Jean Wilhelma in November. She continued John's plan for a wider use of the house, holding three annual conferences there for Quaker and Adult School purposes (a considerable effort for a naturally shy person), and giving holidays to people who needed but couldn't afford them. She worked as a Poor Law Guardian and spent long afternoons cutting out and repairing materials for winter clothes. She often walked or cycled into Scarborough rather than use a carriage. She took an active part in the life of the Meeting and was made an elder though she rarely spoke. She managed the affairs of the house and farm with quiet competence, and made her home a happy place in which to work and live, providing a background of discipline, happiness and security for her children and striving to keep the idea of their father always in their lives without any loss of reality, even for the daughter who had never known him.

Many tributes were paid to John Wilhelm Rowntree, sometimes in extravagant language, and his memory has come to be revered in Quaker circles. But Connie disliked the idolising of her husband as some kind of prophet: he was more complex, more human and more fun than that.

Jean Wilhelma Rowntree b. 1905
about three years old

Description of Holidays in Switzerland, 1884 and 1885

1. A Visit to the Cathedral at Lucerne

We enter, not to see the building, but to hear an organ famed as one of the finest in Europe. The performance in the afternoon, which is entirely for the benefit of visitors who flock to hear it, is wonderfully fine, and, some say, surpasses that which we hear in our own Minster. . . . At one moment scarcely audible, like the sound of distant sighing – then gradually increasing in volume, as if the band of singers was approaching the listener – then dying away like a gentle breeze – a silence – and again a slight whisper of music, a tremulous foreshadowing of something more, a muttering, a hesitation, a grumbling and then a crash! a peal! of music falls on the stunned ear and arouses the utmost echoes of the roof. Suddenly the thunder ceases, a gentle music fills the air, light and fleeting; then more serious and yet louder, till with a solemn tone a peal as of the last trump rings through and through the building; not awful like the last, not a crash but a solemn peal. This peal generally closes the performance which lasts perhaps an hour.

2. An Ascent of Schilthorn

Leaving the others I put on a spirt and reached the top of the mountain alone, before the clouds but only just before. I was surrounded by peaks and summits, and between myself and them deep fathomless abysses. From all sides the clouds were pouring over the mountains, forming rapidly out of nothing in the valleys, meeting and advancing with a rapid noiseless rush towards me where I stood alone. Peak after peak, summit after summit vanished in a black pall, valley after valley wrapped itself in cloud, and then a rush of icy cold air chilled my limbs; another moment and all was darkness. I could see nothing but the snow sloping downward on every side for a few paces and then swallowed up in gloom. But I had not long to wait before dim figures gradually gaining form in the surrounding mist appeared and the pleasant sound of human voices fell on my ears. . . . We decided a descent would be the better part of valour as the thunder was now so ominous. We determined on a glissade and in another moment were whirling down the mountain side.

His other essays in Bootham's *Observer* are:

(a) A day on Lake Como

(b) De Kelto Resuscitante, aliter xxiv pages of pure and original NONSENSE *not* founded on fact. (A fantasy about an ancient Briton sent to sleep on Clifton Ings for 2,000 years, waking up and appearing in modern York.)

(c) A Court of Justice and what there befell. (A fantasy about a flight to the moon where the hero is put on trial as the cow in 'The Cow jumped over the Moon'.)

———

APPENDIX B

Liquorice and Lemon Pastilles

To make a 12 cwt. Mixing

GUM

First take 134lbs of <u>dark gum</u> (price 130/- cwt) and place it in a steam jacketed pan (made of copper and heated by steam) in which <u>108lbs of water</u> are boiling. Immediately on adding the gum, shut off steam. Now stir regularly and continuously (not

115

too fast) with a wooden 'spatter' (spatula) or pole flattened at the end which is immersed. . This stirring prevents the gum from forming in a cake against the sides of the pan and burning. When thoroughly melted the gum will be very <u>thin</u>. This allows the <u>fine sand</u> which is generally found in connection with gum in more or less large quantities <u>to settle</u>. It is for this reason that 108 lbs of water are added.

When the gum is thoroughly melted ladle it out very carefully with a <u>copper ladle</u>, through a <u>copper</u> wire sieve (mesh 22 to inch) into a zinc-plated iron receptacle of any convenient shape or size. If the gum is difficult to work through the sieve, use a blunt-edged <u>copper spade</u> working it up and down on the upper side of the sieve and taking care to hold the spade upright. This operation should be performed in the afternoon, and when the gum has been transferred from the pans into the zinc-plated receptacle, it is left absolutely untouched and still all night.

The result of this is that at 6 o'clock next morning a <u>scum</u> ¼ to ½ an inch in thickness will have formed, and this has to be removed with a copper skimmer, bored with about ⅛ inch holes. When this scum has been removed the gum is poured back into the steam-jacketed boiling-pan before mentioned, through the same copper sieve and in the same manner.

J.W.R. goes on in the same detail to describe the adding of sugar and syrup, glucose and gelatine, and then of liquorice and lemon essence. Later he gives the treatment of the mixing in Henderson's Division in The Starch Room, where the mixing is poured into tins, and in The Stove where the trays are taken for the sweets to set.

(From Volume 1 of Notes written by John Wilhelm Rowntree, and marked PRIVATE.)

———

A Climb in the Alps: the final stage

WE HAD GONE only a very little way when Peter [their guide] suddenly stopped in his work and glanced hastily up at the rocks above the couloir. A second after there was a booming sound like the report of some big gun, and down the other side, or rather down a sort of second couloir, huge rocks came bounding and crashing, followed by a deafening roar which reverberated again and again among the cliffs. We stood perfectly still during this cannonade, as if paralysed, and it was evident that Peter did not care for it, for no sooner had the last shower of rocks rattled into the background than he set himself to work with a will, making the ice fly up on all sides under his powerful blows. Every now and then he stopped to look up and I could see he was anxious to leave the couloir as soon as possible.

Since the fall of this rock avalanche our conversation had practically ceased and I began to wish I was back at the inn. To begin with the slope was so slippery and so steep that it was by no means certain whether, if anyone should fall, the others could stand the jerk, and if they did not and we all went sliding down, there was that horrible bergschrund at the bottom waiting to receive us. After some considerable time, and after we had ascended to a great height we at last, much to my relief, took to the rocks.

But here, however, climbing was difficult and precipitous, and the rope, which Peter would not allow us to dispense with, kept getting in the way in a most aggravating manner. We had been working round more and more to the right ever since leaving the snow, and to my great disgust I saw above me another couloir steeper even than the last. I was getting most decidedly nervous, but still determined to keep on, and it was not till we were all on the ice and cutting steadily up, still to the right, that I really lost self-control.

I had been absorbed in watching Peter, in order to keep pace with his cutting, but he being engaged in making a double step at the corner of a zigzag, I looked up for a moment. I then noticed that the rocks were no longer below us but that the snow which sloped rapidly away from my feet came to a sudden termination, apparently in mid-air. Of course I knew by this that we were above a precipice and the giddiness of the position brought on the attack of vertigo which rendered progress highly unpleasant. Mr Graham's cheery remarks kept up my sinking courage till we reached the end of the snow, when, after a little more rock climbing, we came to a ledge of soft shale where I was unroped and left to myself.

I soon came round a bit, and after eating several prunes, felt myself well enough to proceed. Accordingly when the party returned from the summit Peter and I roped ourselves together and went up alone. The top is scarcely an agreeable position for a long stay or for a large party; indeed it is nothing less than an overhanging wreath of snow, through which I could see a stream far below. I cast a hasty and nervous glance around at the scenery and after remaining there the fraction of a minute, came down to find the others on the ledge, taking a mean advantage of our absence, absorbed in violent and futile endeavours to consume the remainder of the provisions without our help.

A large supply of chicken and prunes drove away my fears, and at half-past twelve we retraced our steps. Fortunately for the party I suffered no uneasiness, and the only adventures were on the first couloir, where I was seized with cramp, and where Mr Graham's step broke under his feet on turning a corner. His exclamation as he began sliding down warned me in time and I brought him up. The jerk had, however, upset my equilibrium, and if it had not been for Peter, I should most infallibly have gone.

No such ill-luck, however, awaited us, and though subjected to rain, hail, thunder and lightning which broke upon us on the Petersgrat and followed us home, we arrived safe, wet and hungry, at our inn somewhere between six and seven in the evening.

(From a lecture on an ascent of Tschingel Horn to York Adult School, 2nd September 1887.)

A Letter to his cousin Arnold Rowntree
on his 21st birthday

30 St Mary's
York

December 4, 1893

My Dear Arno,

Twenty first birthdays are occasions when the victim lays himself open to be lectured – so at least according to my own experience. After all, however, there are times in a man's life which seem to mark the journey as milestones do a road. There is a solemnity in the close of a definite period in life – the entrance upon a new and more responsible future.

One feels – not as Wordsworth puts it 'the shades of the prison house' closing upon us – rather it is the growing sense of life's reality and purpose. We grow graver as we get older. Experience has hard knocks for us that shake the scales from our eyes and force us to look the great facts of eternity fairly and squarely in the face. Each year helps us to shift our values – we only learn by our lives what is real and true.

I have passed some of the milestones that are still for you to pass – I have had one hard knock at least since the careless schooldays and I feel somewhat 'drawn in sympathy to thee' to speak after the manner of an older generation. I hope with all my heart that the road you travel will be a happy one. Not happy in the small sense however – but happy in the highest realisation of the best powers in you – powers of usefulness, powers of helpfulness, powers of sympathy and love.

I don't think I want greater happiness for you than that men shall say of you

> He has done the work of a true man.
> He forgot his own soul for others;
> Himself to his neighbours lending
> He found the Lord in his suffering brothers
> And not in the clouds descending.

Myself I feel to be miserably incomplete – my life feels far from the Divine Harmony – but I can at least feel the greatness of one common need and share with you the longing for

> God's love – unchanging, pure and true
> The Paradise white-shining through
> His peace, the fall of Hermon's dew!

It is a platitude to say that the world needs workers – superfluous to say that the world needs you – that the Society needs you and such like you. I know you are awake to the work that awaits to be done – to the need of our time – to the need for men to lift up the cross of self denial and make Christianity more than ever before a living and a real force to the people of this land – and I know you are a good fellow with a good heart and it is a stimulation and encouragement to fellows like yourself to know you and to feel that you are one who has dedicated his life to the highest service.

I expect in the nature of things my work must increasingly lie in narrower bounds and yours in wider, but always you have my heartfelt sympathy in what you do and always I wish you in the fullest meaning of the words God Speed.

Your very affectionate cousin,

John

———

APPENDIX E

Notes for an Adult School Lesson

(January 6th, 1901 – Leeman Road and Acomb)

Mark vi. 29-46 (Jesus withdrawing from the crowds)
Discuss verses. (Introductory).
Withdrawal, not of sympathy, but of self.

Need amid thronging events for retirement.

Mount Hermon, uplands, Hauran, the lake, the twinkling lights of cities by the sea.

Panorama – spiritual panorama. . . .

The beginning of a new century is an opportunity for retirement to the mountain for prayer. It does not necessarily close or open an epoch. 18th century lived on to the thirties, next epoch closed in the eighties. But seeing there are such occasions, may as well use them, even if artificial.

Draw first two brief contrasts – religious and social.

1 Social

Gradual deterioration since Elizabeth.
Improvement in middle of 18th century.
Two important changes. WAR. INDUSTRIAL REVOLUTION
Chronic scarcity and growing pauperism.
Wheat 108s per quarter, 1795. . . .

1800. Combination Act. Absolutely forbade any combination for higher wages or fewer hours. The working class was unrepresented. Even the Reform Bill merely gave more power to the upper and middle classes.

The golden age of the capitalist.

Napoleonic Wars cost £800,000,000.

Everything was taxed, even bricks, stones, glass, hats, etc.

Food was dear. In these terrible circumstances of war, heavy taxation and pauperism, modern industry had birth. . . . Development of agitation and legislation.

Franchise, education, material improvements of travel, three days versus three hours to London, telegraph, gas, electricity.

Cheapening and freedom of press. (Once a tax of 4d on each paper.)

Sydney Webb has drawn impressive picture of change.

1851. Amalgamation of engineering societies gave great impetus.

Now 1,800,000 members of trade unions and 3¼ million of money. . . .

Turn briefly to religion.

Calvinism – almost universal in influence.

Election and rejection. God as a Grand Turk. Hell fires.

Rousseau and French Revolution.

Robert Burns' 'A Man's a man for a' that'.

Calvinism – a religion of privilege. . . .

Darwin and Evolution.

Ideas in melting pot. Escape from a gloomy creed had not yet led us to accept positive faith. . . .

Uncertainty of outlook.

Rule over 400,000,000 persons. Football, sport, comic papers.

Imperialism, – i.e. bigness. Bishop of Hereford on little nations.

Greece. Athens smaller than County of Glamorgan.

> 'Her citizens, imperial spirits,
> Rule the present from the past;
> On all this world of men inherits
> Their seal is set.'

Florence smaller than Bolton; Venice smaller than Salford.

Impossible to say what is to be the line of progress. Some say democracy – some say not. One thing clear.

Decline of British supremacy in trade – greatness shall not rest on bigness. America produces double iron and steel of England. Last year her coal output exceeded ours. Other nations making their own and improving quality.

On what shall our national greatness rest? On character. Personal thoughts.

Whatever factory legislation, etc., may do – it can do nothing unless character is ennobled

In this sense take the opportunity, now that the evening of the old century has gone, and go up alone into the mountain and pray.

A few Thoughts upon the Position of Young Friends in Relation to the Society

THE SUBJECT of the state of the Society of Friends in respect of its younger members had been very much on my mind before the Yearly Meeting. Since the sittings on May 25th and 26th, when such a loving spirit was manifested, I have felt that a few thoughts on the subject which I had transferred to paper before Yearly Meeting might still serve some purpose, if only by eliciting a free interchange of opinion. These thoughts are based only on what I know of meetings in the North of England, and I am anxious to make it understood that I write not in a spirit of criticism, but rather to set forth some of the difficulties and wants felt by very many of us as young Friends.

I have experienced for some time and have seen in others a more or less vague sense of want and dissatisfaction in connection with our worship and the condition of our Meetings. (I have felt)

(a) a want of harmony with the older generation, their modes of expression and thought, involving misunderstandings perhaps on both sides,

(b) a fear on the part of many young Friends that what are sometimes spoken of as 'unsound views' would not be sympathetically understood, but would meet with suspicion and aversion, and a consequent tendency on their part towards not doing anything so far as work and ministry in the Society are concerned,

(c) a large amount of spiritual lukewarmness, together with much worldliness.

These points have seemed to me to weaken the ties which bind such as myself to the Society. Things have been made singularly easy and fortunate for me in York, but I have been increasingly impressed with the extent to which these conditions apply to others. Young Friends who, though earnest and sincerely seeking to live a true life and to follow more closely the example of Jesus, find themselves, from no intellectual arrogance, but in real humility of spirit, looking at truth from a different standpoint from that of many older Friends. My near acquaintance, scattered pretty widely over the country, find that their aspect of truth differs more or less from that commonly put forward in meeting. The recent Yearly Meeting discussion on the state of the Society has given us a future full of hope – there is a broader and more sympathetic tone prevalent. It is not the expectation of those for whom I speak that the older generation should see with our eyes. We are anxious not to dwell on the differences in our points of vision, and only ask for a liberal measure of Christian tolerance on both sides. . . .

There is much of the ministry that expresses itself in an habitual phraseology which to young minds is almost a dead language. There is much that confines itself too narrowly to the Bible for its incidents, illustration and quotation. The Bible incidents are many of them so well worn and the thoughts that derive from them travel on such beaten tracks that I have often after listening to the opening remarks of some Friend found myself correctly forecasting the entire drift of what followed and as often unable even to maintain attention. A recognition of the real value of modern literature and historical biblical criticism would breath new life into many of the old scenes and characters. Hardly anything could come home to us more than simple instances taken from our own times of the effect of Christian love upon those who come under its influence. To satisfy intellectual needs, I am certain that the speaker who will from time to time clothe his thoughts in the language of some modern thinker or poet, will do much to enrich a meeting. Many of us cannot think that the inspiration and messages of God have ceased with the Bible, and we feel that to be denied in our meetings for worship the beautiful expression given to the truths of God by men like Browning, Tennyson and our own Whittier is but an impoverishment. . . .

An occasional address, practical and uncontroversial, on these lines will do much to increase the sense of harmonious purpose and will come like rain on desert places. I believe too that such an address may be an encouragement to a young Friend to say what he has in his heart without feeling that his words would be incongruous or out of place in the meeting because not couched in any set phrases or dealing with any fine point of theology. I entirely feel the force of what an older Friend once said to me that we younger Friends must take our part as being best able to deal with some of the needs of those near us in age.

Take the case of a young Friend who, not from shallowness or cynicism but from an earnest desire to realise practically in his own life the teaching and example of Jesus, had been compelled to change his point of view, and suppose him to hear an honest search for truth spoken of only with bitterness or as a temptation of the devil, is it not 10 chances to one that he should feel chilled? Would he not feel himself outcast, suspect? The Yearly Meeting has expressed warm sympathy for those in this position, and if this sympathy be shown in the right way, great benefit will result. But sympathy must not take the form of pity. I recollect reading a letter from an old lady Friend to a friend of mine who had been compelled in sincerity to change his thoughts on matters of belief. This letter was evidently written from the heart and with great tenderness but nevertheless had just the opposite effect to that desired. It showed entire inability to understand the other side, expressing pity and a certainty that the wanderer would return. Such a letter, though written in the kindliest spirit, produced, as I know, hopelessness of the possibility of harmony and fostered the idea of ultimate severance from the Society.

The mistake is often made of assuming that change in the form of belief is necessarily destructive and cannot be constructive; and such terms as 'wandering in the mists of doubt', 'spiritual blindness', etc. are used of many who feel on the contrary that to them has come a clear vision and the dawn of a brighter day. So long as our religion is the same and difference lies in the thoughts that clothe our religion alone, so long as we have an earnest desire to know God and to express our knowledge of him practically in daily life, surely there is sufficient basis of harmony to enable us to live together to our mutual benefit. To me it would seem sad if it were so, if such as myself were unable to find a home in our Society and were to live debarred from entering the many services of our body that afford scope for those whose hearts (no matter what their creed) are warmed for a work of love. It would seem sad too, if, departing from the example of earlier Friends, we demanded that all thought should conform to a cast-iron model and should refuse to give scope to all who, obeying faithfully that light which they have, are unable to accept many theological dogmas. . . . A correspondent of mine, writing on this point, has said that if we waited until we are sure of everything before we could work, we should waste half of our lives, and if we cannot accept truth second-hand but claim to be taught of God alone, the older generation must be patient with us if we are slow.

Surely the lines divergent today are the more likely to grow one, if such an active life finds its scope within the Society rather than outside it, in contact with those whose thoughts differ from ours rather than in separation. A life of joint purpose will, I believe, be fruitful of blessing, whatever the measure of intellectual agreement attained.

Address to the Manchester Conference –
Has Quakerism a Message to the World Today?

THIS QUESTION has been answered in the affirmative by those who have preceded me. But the possession of a message is one thing, and its delivery to the age another. I therefore propose to consider three great prevailing elements which we must take into account:–

> Indifference to the Higher Life
> The change in Religious Thought
> The expansion of social ideals.

Sadly we must admit that in the cities of modern civilisation the tide of paganism still runs high. The growing magnificence of our public houses and music-halls, and the large and flourishing fraternity of sporting papers are but an index to the power of low ideals over the minds of men. The greed for wealth, the tyranny of drink, the passion for gambling, the fascinations of vice, these have too often in the past baffled the endeavour of reforming zeal.

But it is not only with an *active* hostility that we have to cope. The Church, in her appeal to the conscience of men, meets with no more frequent or obstinate difficulty than that of indifference to the higher life. Who has not seen the spectacle, so pathetic and so common, of the man with the muck-rake, absorbed body and soul in scraping together his little heap of gold? Who has not observed the vulgar and selfish display of the 'nouveau riche', or the less vulgar but no less selfish uselessness of the mere dilettante, who dabbles in art and indulges in travel, not that he may brighten the lives of others, but only to gratify himself? Who does not know the large class, indolently benevolent and negatively virtuous, who, wanting in the depth of conviction, offer a passive obstruction to the progress of the Church? Alas for the army of the Lord, when men desert the rough life of the soldier and the rude ways of the camp for the pleasant and sheltered streets of Laodicea!

The opposition of indifference is, however, no new thing. It is when we pass from indifference to the mental atmosphere of our day that we meet with conditions which, save for the striking period of the Renaissance, find no parallel in history. Great was then the expansion of human knowledge, but to us it has been given to apply the invisible forces of nature, and almost to annihilate time and space. And as the Middle Ages learnt the place of the earth in the universe, so we are learning the truth about man, his slow development, his physical affinities with all other forms of life.

We too have to reconstruct our cosmogony. And in this reconstruction the timidity of the Church, the irreconcilable attitude of certain among our scientists and the revulsion from the iron hardness of terrible and fatalistic creeds have led to some present confusion. There are, it is true, many whom nothing has yet troubled and over whom, no doubt, the Church maintains her hold. But nevertheless, where in any place the Church has failed to grasp the changed conditions, she suffers continued defections and ceases to appeal to an ever increasing number outside her borders. Many churches are enfeebled, many find themselves forced to exchange wholesome centres of activity for the misery of spiritual loneliness and must drift to extremes of negation or seek relief in isolated service.

God's secrets are often swiftly unveiled. But though the revelation may be sudden, our re-adjustment is slow. Confusion, nevertheless, is not for ever. One moment the Bible seems taken from us, the next it is restored, more living than before and with a new light on its page. The clouds of controversy gather at each great discovery of science and seem to hide the Christ; but lo! the clouds disperse and the Divine figure stands out in renewed splendour. Even as now, so at the Renaissance came perplexity and scepticism. But it was of the new learning, with its larger views of God and the universe, that the reformation was born. So do I unfalteringly believe will there spring out of the present seeming chaos a renewed and more powerful faith, deeper in its basis, clearer in its vision, broader in its charity than ever was the old, *and as warm in its love.*

We have now briefly dwelt on two of our three conditions – Indifference to the Higher Life and the change in Religious Thought. Closely allied to this last – which is after all only an inevitable development of the Reformation, accelerated and illumined by scientific discovery – we find a great expansion of social ideals. No one could fail to note how swift and momentous has been the industrial revolution of the past 100 years. The creation of our great industrial classes, the massing together of men in huge centres such as London, Birmingham and Manchester has altered the whole fabric of society and forces of unknown power are coming into play. The progress of political enfranchisement has almost completely transferred the governing power to the hands of the people and the increasing efficiency of education must inevitably tend to bring the humblest citizen and the humblest peasant to political consciousness.

Already there are signs of movement in the deep. The supposed immutability of the existing social system is questioned. Men even doubt if it can be the best. They refuse to believe *that* to be an ideal life which compels the labourer 'to hold desperately to the small niche into which he has been fitted, if he would not be of the helpless flotsam and jetsam tossed to and fro on the tides of poverty'. They refuse the comfortable belief that the present extreme inequalities of wealth are the ordering of Divine providence or that the strong caste feeling that mars English social life reflects the teaching of the Nazarene Joiner.

The profound dissatisfaction with existing conditions and the desire for a fuller and a happier life are well nigh universal. But still it is true that 'there is an almost complete absence of any clear indication from those who speak in the name of science and authority as to the direction in which the path of future progress lies'. There are those who think the outlook is already brightening with the light of a better day. That may well be true, but it would be idle to maintain that the situation is not fraught with danger. 'We see not our signs. There is no more any prophet.' Let us listen then to the warning voice of perhaps the greatest of our Nonconformist leaders: 'We are face to face with what we may truly call the supreme moment of our history. It is the people that now rule, and unless *God* live in and through the people, the end of all our struggles, the goal of all our boasted progress will be chaos, and chaos is death.'

These three elements: Indifference to the Higher Life, the Change in Religious Thought and the Expansion of Social Ideals must be vividly realised if we would make our appeal a message to the world today. And I am thankful that Friends, having caught something of the spirit that was in their greatest leaders, have met at this Conference boldly to face facts and frankly review their position. Never, it has been said, in spite of all that is discouraging, was an age more earnest in spirit, an age so moved and so possessed with the consciousness of evil. And though this earnestness may be largely outside the initiative of the Church, it is an element of the highest promise of good. This is no place for pessimism. 'He shall not fail nor be discouraged till he hath set judgement in the earth.'

Yet we cannot look unmoved at the extent to which the Churches generally, not least our own, fail to inspire and lead the people. Can we really say that they hold men as they did? We cannot believe it. It needs but the briefest acquaintance with our large cities to reveal the existence among the people of widespread mistrust of Church and Chapel. And in considering the number of their adherents we are bound to remember that the census of a Church is but a deceptive index of its spiritual power. We must deduct those who from the force of habit rather than from strength of conviction or from love of respectability rather than that of truth cumber the pews with a soulless occupancy. The large activity which spends itself in Bazaar Committees, or the proud charity that loves the high places of subscription lists, is no criterion of deep religious feeling.

If there be failure, the cause must be sought, not without the Church, but *within*. The empty benches and deserted galleries of our meeting-houses are signs of a high-water mark from which the tide has ebbed away. We may recognise local or particular reasons, more or less pertinent, but the real causes, which cannot be minimised, are the poverty of our spiritual life or the want of aggressive power. Were the simple worship of those who profess to go beneath form and convention and strike deep springs of actual communion with the Father to become only another of the empty forms of religion, then grant us another George Fox to denounce us as 'professors'! Our meetings for worship must be glowing centres of our spiritual life if we could keep and attract men or satisfy their spiritual hunger.

I believe it is sadly too true that spiritual pride, false respectability and unmanly deference to mere wealth or title have crept into our Church; and wherever they are still to be found we see the melancholy spectacle of an invertebrate Christianity, which in its sluggish self-complacency is even ignorant of its weakness. A lady recently told me, 'I had thought of becoming a Friend, but I found you were a pearl of such great price that I had not the spiritual pride to join you.' Such is not the attitude for an appeal to the world. As labourers seeking help to carry on a great work, for which our strength is inadequate, it is both our right and our duty to call men to us, and in the plea that 'we are not a proselytising body' there lies the poison of stagnation. Rather let us break down our barriers and offer our fellow-workers a social and a spiritual home.

To the true Christian the world is a commonwealth of all men, knowing neither rank nor class. Nevertheless certain sections of the Christian Church tend to represent certain grades of society and to perpetuate class distinctions rather than destroy them. The equality of position nominally possessed by our members should remind us that we are bound, more than other churches, to overcome this difficulty. There is however grave danger of one-sidedness. We shall never know our full power if we appeal to the working class alone. Why do we fail almost entirely to reach cultured and thoughtful people? Why is it that even many of our own more educated members are leaving us? By all means let us encourage the Adult School movement, and let us welcome every working man who comes into membership with us, but we must remember that our message is for the world. True thought clearly and simply expressed reaches all men. It is a great mistake to imagine that what satisfies the simplest may not also be food for the most completely furnished minds.

Surely it is impossible to view without concern the spiritual starvation of our professional and literary classes. Great is the talent committed to their charge and small the use they make of it. Would they but contribute to religion something nobler than fastidious criticism of other men's methods, they could render the Church a powerful service of trained intelligence, which she greatly needs. *How* to set free their dormant spiritual energy is a problem demanding from us all the self sacrifice and patient thought that have characterised our devotion to our Adult Schools. And though, hitherto, it has been strangely neglected, it is a work which if more difficult is no less urgent. I do not suggest the method, but though there are many Adult Schools in London, I know of none in Fleet Street for lawyers and journalists, and none in Piccadilly for baronets and dukes. But because these men are difficult to reach, we have no right to shrink from our duty. Difficulties exist to be overcome. And were there more of that close dependence on God and fearless independence of men which marked John Woolman and Stephen Grellet, we should not stand under the condemnation of this failure.

Let us welcome a large conception of our responsibilities. Great hearted men are not nurtured on small ideals, and there is something in our Church of that parochialism which is fatal to vigorous action. Parochialism and exclusiveness bring with them that want of proportion so typical of Friends. Such a matter as the sitting together of men and women Friends in Meeting is surely of infinitesimal importance when measured by the larger concerns of life. Yet I have heard that petty question discussed in a usually torpid Preparative Meeting with the heat and passion of a House of Commons debate. If we are to do great things we must lift up our eyes from our microscopic affairs and look out upon the world. And if we look aright we shall see – across the darkness of vice unconquered and problems unsolved – like a vision of the Holy Grail, the city of God that is to be, and into our souls will come a great longing, and to our ears the sound of a voice, 'Arise and labour, for the need is great'.

Is there development in Social Ideals? Then let us face the facts, nor lose our faith in the power of true religion to guide and inspire. Christianity is before all things practical. A presentment of truth merely theological is also inadequate. We shall give more force to the preaching of Christ if we illustrate our theology by our practice, and work with a deep sense of our social responsibility. Let working men feel our sympathy as something more than a kind of patronage, let them feel that we believe in brotherhood, not as a mere catch-word but as an essential teaching of Christ. Let them see that irresponsible and selfish wealth, blind to its potentialities for good, has our scornful and pitying denunciation, and we shall do something to dispel their justifiable distrust. The message of salvation hereafter is cold comfort to men who are starving here; and it is our place as soldiers of the Cross to bring hope and gladness into barren places and to carry the glad presence of the living Christ into dark slums and lonely garrets. The engineer is helpless without *applied mechanics*, and if we Adult School teachers would bridge the gulf between rich and poor, we must study the dark problems of poverty which cry aloud for solution and give our teaching the force of APPLIED CHRISTIANITY.

Is there change and perplexity in Religious Thought? Let us face the facts with confidence and courage. If the age of the faith which comes by tradition and authority is gone and men can no longer believe without knowing why they believe; if they are expanding those partial views of the truth that were inevitable in earlier times, then such a change will bring as its ultimate result not weakness but new strength. At the root of this great movement is the longing for reality, for a more real and human touch with God. We must not – we dare not – continue in a spirit of timid conservatism. We must understand sympathetically if we would convince and lead. Those who, having the ability, refuse to acquaint themselves with the modern development of thought, sadly limit the scope of their service. That faith alone will satisfy which, triumphant and aggressive, fights no longer with 'bows and arrows, but arms her with the weapons of the time'.

In the early days faith and science were one. What we wait for now is a religion that shall once more appeal to the whole complex nature of man. Much earnest Christianity today fails to command the intellect and establish its own authority beyond all doubt and criticism. Yet a religion merely intellectual will never warm the heart with the fire of self-sacrificing love. Let us in our message offer that which is beyond all creeds – the evidence in our lives of communion with the spirit of God. The need of positive animating faith in the inward presence of His spirit was never greater than now. All who earnestly seek truth could unite with us in fellowship on the broad platform of faith in that indwelling guidance. The Church exists to create for each succeeding generation the ideal of the

Christ in the thought-form of the age, and in the adaptability of Christ's teaching lies one secret of its power. Friends are not bound by a heritage of creeds, and need not break with their great past to put themselves in touch with the present.

Is there perplexity and change in religious thought? Then God grant to our Church the spirit of understanding which shall give her the eye of a seer, the voice of a prophet, the place and power of a leader.

Is there Indifference to the Higher Life? Then, O Christ, convince us by thy spirit, thrill us with thy divine passion, drown our selfishness in thy invading love, lay on us the burden of the world's suffering, drive us forth with the apostolic fervour of the early Church! So only can our message be delivered:– 'Speak to the Children of Israel, that they go forward.'

———

APPENDIX H

Hannah Doncaster's description
of a young Friend of 1895

LET US SUPPOSE the instance of a young man Friend coming fresh from school or college, and at his father's works getting to know the workmen, and meeting practically with many of the great social problems of the day. Well for him if he does not give up the solution in despair, he all inexperienced as he is and one little unit in this seething mass of humanity. How comfortable to forget it all, to decide that we may as well enjoy what we have, for if we gave it up it would only get into worse hands; and even if given to the deserving it is but as nothing compared with the great need. How easy for our young Friend to decide upon philanthropic work in the town and to be a just master, but that the social problem is too great for him.

If he falls into this frame of mind he may remain a member of the Society of Friends, but he is turning his back upon one great part of its mission at the present day. But if he sets himself to work to see what he, unit though he be, can do to help on the better social system which he feels is possible, he will find one organisation in our midst, that of our Adult Schools, where all meet on an equality. He takes a Sunday class in an Adult School, and from the study of the Bible endeavours with the men around him to find out how to live a practical Christian life. He also becomes initiated into the various outside organisations of the School.

Yet still, let us hope, he is not satisfied. He goes to his home, leaving the toilers and the smoke behind him. He looks at his bookshelves filled with valuable books, at his room hung with pictures, at his cabinet stored with treasures, and the thought of those men in his class comes over him. He remembers the eagerness of some of them to improve upon their scanty education; of their self-sacrifice in order to give their children more advantages than they have had. A feeling of deep humiliation fills his heart and he cannot bear to have so much more of the good things of life than his toiling brothers and sisters. Then the thought comes suddenly to him, 'I have these things, why not share them?' It is a new life to him. All that hitherto he has delighted in for its own sake, he finds has now an added charm when used for others.

The results of the intercourse which our young Friend has with his class outside the Bible lesson are far greater than he in his humility can imagine. The men who have hitherto thought of those possessed of means as selfish and grasping will begin to see very differently. They will learn that many who seem to shut themselves up with their possessions only want the knowledge of how to share them. Our young Friend himself will find that the workmen whom formerly he thought envious and intolerant show no jealousy of him; and on both sides class distinctions and misunderstandings will disappear and in their place lasting friendships will be formed. In this softening process true brotherhood, such as Christ taught, will grow to be a reality with them, and through it they will learn more and more of the love of the universal Father.

Report of the Manchester Conference, pp 184-5.

Two lectures on Art (Selected Paragraphs)

I. The Place of Art in Religion and Life

A CERTAIN OXFORD DON, whose nervousness in society occasionally disturbed the felicity of his speech, is reported to have said to a guest who seemed about to hint at departure *'Can't* you go, *must* you stay?' I have an uncomfortable suspicion that this sentiment, concealed no doubt by a considerable delicacy, is widely represented in my audience. The best defence I can make is one so often made before magistrates (of course I do not mean in *that* case by me) and also I believe by unsuccessful performers on the stage – that this will *positively* be my last appearance.

As this is the case it is my duty to gather up the threads and to tie them together in a final and effective knot. Let us briefly summarise.

In our first lecture we examined the early German and Flemish prints, both the Helgen or Holy pictures, the block-books and the general book illustrations of the 15th century. In these we found evidence of what we described as the childhood of faith. In Albrecht Dürer's Apocalypse we saw the revolt of piety from the views of a church grown formal and hypocritical; in his Melancholia we saw the travail of the soul under the stress of life's great enigma; and in the Knight, Sin and Death, the victorious issue.

Turning to Holbein we traced the emancipation of art and faith from ecclesiastical dominion culminating in that fine charter of liberty, the print of the True Light. Lastly we saw in the Dance of Death the failure of a pagan culture that was not rooted in the knowledge and love of God.

Tonight by way of exordium we will devote some time to French and Italian prints, which we have as yet entirely overlooked and by way of conclusion extract the moral, not of any particular lecture but of their sum.

Of the exordium Italy must have the lion's share, and France, I fear, in spite of the entente cordiale so welcome to all true lovers of liberty, equality and brotherhood, and in spite of the great debt we owe to her in art and letters, must receive the briefest though I trust an honourable mention.

In French engraving then, at the close of the 15th century and the opening of the 16th century, we find ourselves, as in Germany, in a purely religious atmosphere. We are at Lyons, to the world of books in the West, what Venice was in the East. The Israelites are on the march – a mighty host winding through the bare defiles of Sinai. Woe! to Canaan when this wave breaks upon its shores. And the artist is Salomon, he who played Elisha to Holbein's Elijah. but Elisha was not as great as Elijah. There is much ineffective work in Salomon, who had yielded to the prevailing tendency to imitate copper-plates on wood. Between 1545 and 1580 more books containing small wood-cuts were printed at Lyons than in any other city or town in Europe, during the corresponding period. It was the grand market for scripture cuts, emblems and devices, but out of the many hundreds of engravings it would be difficult to select 20 that are really excellent. . . .

II. The Laws of Beauty

THE THEORY I have to propound is as follows:– In early days man had an instinctive perception of the beautiful. More then than now he was a child of nature, he lived closer to her harmonies, more clearly heard her sweet music. The growth of civilisation did not interfere with this instinctive perception so long as it accomplished the moral development of the nation or race. Greece rose to heights not reached before or since. . . . But decline in Grecian art ultimately meant the decline morally and politically of Greece itself. . . . Look at the revival of Florentine art rising Phoenix-like from the ashes of classic antiquity – it was bound up with religious life of the time, and its decline was also the decline of the church of Rome.

To come to 1860, the apotheosis of English vulgarity. The steam engine, locomotive and stationary, had brought about the greatest economic disturbance the world has ever seen. Only now are we recovering from the blow. Steadily perception of beauty is being recovered and bitter experience having taught us lessons, we shall find, not that we can do as well as those of the ancients who caught the hem of beauty's fleeting robes, but better.

*Graves of John Wilhelm Rowntree and Rufus M. Jones
in the Friends Burial Ground, Haverford, Pennsylvania, USA (see p. xii)*

Index

138